HAPPY
BIRTHDAY
TIM!
HAPPY HIKING!
Love and Hugs

Annie
Franklin
Genna
Tim
Rgney
and
CHum

D1048387

Favorite Wildflower
Walks in Georgia

Favorite Wildflower Walks in Georgia

Hugh Nourse and Carol Nourse

The University
of Georgia Press

Athens and London

© 2007 by The University of Georgia Press
Athens, Georgia 30602
All rights reserved

Designed and composed by Jacky Woolsey,
    Paper Moon Graphics, Inc.
Set in Adobe Garamond Premier Pro
Printed and bound by Kings Time Printing Press

The paper in this book meets the guidelines for permanence
and durability of the Committee on Production Guidelines
for Book Longevity of the Council on Library Resources.

Printed in China

10 09 08 07 06 P 5 4 3 2 1

Library of Congress Cataloging-in-Publication Data
Nourse, Hugh O.
    Favorite wildflower walks in Georgia /
        Hugh Nourse and Carol Nourse.
            p. cm. — (A Wormsloe Foundation nature book)
        Includes bibliographical references and index.
        ISBN-13: 978-0-8203-2841-6 (pbk. : alk. paper)
        ISBN-10: 0-8203-2841-3 (pbk. : alk. paper)
1. Wild flowers—Georgia—Identification.   2. Nature trails—
Georgia—Guidebooks.   3. Georgia—Guidebooks.
I. Nourse, Carol, 1933–   II. Title.
    QK155.N68 2006
    582.1309758—dc22   2006021899

British Library Cataloging-in-Publication Data available

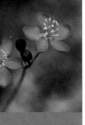

Contents

Piedmont

Coastal Plain

Acknowledgments

Members of the Georgia Botanical Society, particularly their trip chairs and trip leaders, introduced us to most of the places listed in this book, as well as many other unusual botanical areas. The trip leaders include Jim Allison, Alan Bailey, Steve Bowling, Linda Chafin, Hal Massie, Marie Mellinger, Michael Wayne Morris, Fred Parrish, Tom Patrick, Scott Ranger, Rich Reaves, J. P. Schmidt, Albie Smith, and Richard Ware. Special thanks to Tom Patrick, Scott Ranger, and Linda Chafin for help in choosing among the many authorities on plant nomenclature and taxonomy. Leslie Edwards has given us great help in describing the environments. We are grateful for the detailed and thoughtful comments of Jim Allison and Robert Wyatt on several versions of the manuscript. Although we are thankful for all the help we have received, we are responsible for any remaining errors.

Three of these chapters previously appeared in slightly different form in *Wildflower Magazine*: The Tennessee Rock Trail as "Black Rock Mountain State Park," 18.2 (2002); "Cedar Glades," 19.2 (2003); and Jekyll Island as "The Marshes of Glynn and Jekyll Island," 17.3 (2001).

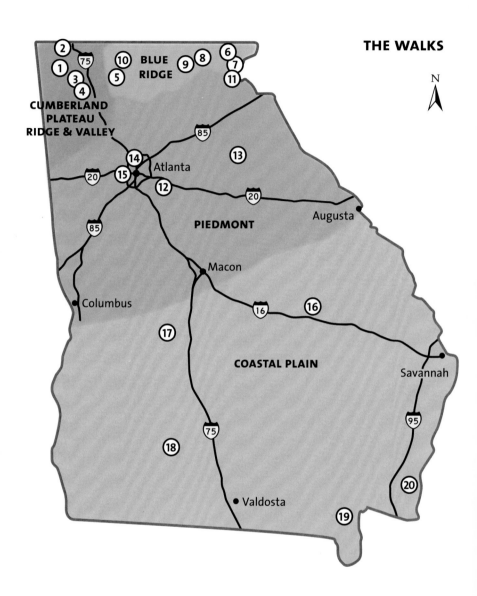

THE WALKS

N

CUMBERLAND
PLATEAU
RIDGE & VALLEY

BLUE
RIDGE

Atlanta

PIEDMONT

Augusta

Macon

Columbus

COASTAL PLAIN

Savannah

Valdosta

Introduction

When we present slide shows about the wildflowers of Georgia, the question most often asked is, "Where can I go to see these flowers?" This book will help you find wildflower walks in diverse habitats in Georgia.

Although the level of discussion is aimed at the novice wildflower enthusiast, we have tried to provide sufficient information to interest more experienced and knowledgeable wildflower fans. Some readers may use this book as a bridge to more technical botany books. Our hope is that an appreciation of Georgia's wildflowers will lead to a desire to support conservation of natural areas in the state.

The walks chosen for this book are all on public land: state and local parks, wildlife management areas, state natural areas, national recreation areas, and so on—with fairly unrestricted public access. They have been selected from our favorite walks in Georgia because of the density or the unusual nature of the floral display to be seen on each walk. We have included five walks from each of the four physiographic regions of the state: Blue Ridge Mountains; Cumberland Plateau/Ridge and Valley; Piedmont; and Coastal Plain (including the barrier islands).

The Blue Ridge Mountains region, which covers the northeastern part of the state, includes Brasstown Bald, the highest point in Georgia at 4,784 feet. The underlying rock in this area is metamorphic, and many members of the heath family thrive in the acidic soils. Some of the richest wildflower communities are in north-facing coves below boulder fields.

The Cumberland Plateau/Ridge and Valley includes the northwestern part of the state. U.S. 411 provides a rough eastern boundary, with the southern boundary just south of Cedartown. The underlying rock here is sedimentary, much of it limestone or sandstone. Plants that like calcium occur more often in the limestone areas. Many plants found here also grow in the prairies of the Midwest, which also have developed almost entirely over sedimentary rock. For example, one of the rarest habitats in this region is the limestone cedar glade, which is more common from Tennessee westward into Missouri.

The Piedmont, literally the "foot of the mountain," includes the rolling hills between the two previous regions and the fall line. This line (more a fuzzy boundary than a line), which runs approximately from Columbus to Macon to Augusta, marks a change from higher to lower elevations and from predominantly red clay to sandy soil. Historically the fall line was the point on navigable streams at which waterfalls prevented further navigation from the coast into the interior. One of the most unusual habitats in the Piedmont of Georgia and other southeastern states is the granitic outcrop, which harbors a unique community of plants that can survive in desertlike conditions amid the oak–hickory–pine forests more typical of the region.

The Coastal Plain comprises the rest of the state below the fall line, land that was formerly continental shelf, beaches, and dunes. The soil tends to be sandy. When naturalist William Bartram adventured here in the 1770s, more than 90 million acres of longleaf pine forest carpeted with wiregrass stretched from Virginia to Texas. Only 3 percent of the original longleaf pine forest is left today. Longleaf pine wiregrass communities contain an astonishing diversity of wildflowers. In poorly drained areas, they may harbor pitcher-plant bogs, spectacular in bloom. This region also includes the fabled barrier islands, or sea islands, on the coast, and Okefenokee Swamp in the southeastern corner of the state.

Some plants grow only in one region, but others grow in

every county in the state. Many Blue Ridge Mountain plants and Coastal Plain plants also grow in the Piedmont. Unusual mixtures of plants occur along the boundary where two regions meet. Still, each of these four regions has its own character.

For each walk we indicate the flowering season, peak flowering times, walk length, walk rating, restroom availability, whether there are fees, directions, and a description of the habitat. We provide a trail map and describe the walk, giving the common names of plants that might be seen at various seasons of the year. In the appendix, we summarize the flowering seasons and peak flowering times for all walks. The index lists (with both common and scientific names) the plants mentioned in the text. The lists are not meant to be a complete plant inventory: not every plant that grows in these areas is mentioned. Besides, plant communities vary from year to year. We are leaving for you the fun of discovering and identifying other flowers in these areas. A general scenic view of part of the walk gives a hint of its character, and five wildflower species, all native to Georgia, on each walk are selected for a photograph and profile. Some rare and endangered wildflowers are included, but most are the more common flowers you are likely to encounter on these and other walks. Information about historic medicinal or culinary uses is intended only as an interesting fact about the plant: we do not encourage you to use the plant in these ways. With more than 3,500 flowering plants in Georgia, we obviously cannot profile all of them, but we hope that knowing their names and something more about these few adds to your enjoyment of their beauty.

These walks are merely an introduction to Georgia's wealth of wildflowers. We hope that you will explore the parks, nature centers, and other natural areas in your neighborhood to discover their treasures, and we hope that you will work to preserve such areas for the enjoyment of future generations of Georgians.

To help you on your path of discovery, we recommend

Duncan and Duncan (1999) for identifying plants. This guidebook includes 630 photos of wildflowers plus descriptive material that increases the number of species that can be identified to about 1,200. Still that is only one-third of the plants found in Georgia, and the book does not include any woody plants, ferns, or vines. Four other field guides cover these additional categories of plants: Brown and Kirkman (1990) or Duncan and Duncan (1988) for trees; Snyder and Bruce (1986) for ferns; and Foote and Jones (1989) for shrubs and vines. When possible, common names used in the text are drawn from these five sources, so that you can easily find in them pictures or line drawings of the plants mentioned. Rickett (1966), not a field guide but an older reference, also includes photographs, so we have used it as a source for common names of plants not covered in the books mentioned above.

The Georgia Botanical Society introduces its members to botanical keys through workshops in which the text is Radford, Ahles, and Bell (1968). Of books in print, it is still a major resource for finding the scientific names of many plants in Georgia, though it was written for the Carolinas. However, since that text was written, botanists have discovered new species in Georgia, have improved keys, and have renamed plants to conform more closely to evolutionary relationships. Fortunately a new source, Weakley (2005), that includes plants in Georgia is now available online. This is our source for the scientific names listed in the text. We list as synonyms the scientific names found in the sources we used for common names, if they differ from those in Weakley.

A note of caution: Carry water and a snack on longer walks. Sunscreen and insect repellent may be needed. The walking paths vary from sidewalks to dirt paths with roots, rocks, and crude stairways, so wear good walking shoes. On specific trails where high water levels can pose problems, we have added warnings.

The threats to wildflower habitats are many: development, encroachment by exotic species, and abuse by foot and vehicular traffic, among others. These areas could be destroyed if people trample on plants, pick flowers, or dig them up. With that in mind, here are some rules, also promoted by the Georgia Botanical Society on its field trips, to guide you in your walks:

- No plant collecting. This is expressly forbidden and illegal in these areas.

- No picking of flowers. This is expressly forbidden and illegal in these areas.

- Stay on trails. We know of plants that have been destroyed by people taking shortcuts on these very walks. Please do not make new paths.

- Don't trample the vegetation.

- Take only pictures and leave only footprints, but also be careful where you leave those footprints!

I

Shirley Miller Wildflower Trail

Crockford–Pigeon Mountain Wildlife Management Area

Flowering Season	March through June
Peak Flowering	Mid-March to Mid-April
Walk Length	Less than 2 miles
Walk Rating	Easy on the boardwalk; moderate on rough trail to falls
Restrooms	None
Fee	None

Directions From LaFayette drive west on Ga. 193 8 miles to Davis Corners. Turn left (south) on Hog Jowl Road. At a fork just past a church (2.5 miles), continue left on Hog Jowl Road. At the top of the hill just after this fork (0.2 mile), turn left on Pocket Road. Continue on this road, which becomes a gravel road, for 1.2 miles to the parking area.

Environment This trail takes you through a cove of mixed mesic hardwoods, with **tuliptree** dominating the canopy. The understory includes **American hornbeam**, **boxelder**, and **yellow buckeye**. The sides of the cove slope steeply to a colluvial plain through which the Pocket Branch flows. The underlying rock here is sedimentary, quite different from the metamorphic rock of the Blue Ridge area in northeastern Georgia. Material from the slopes washes down to the cove floor, bringing with it calcium from limestone in the cliffs and producing nearly neutral rather than acid soils. Plants that prefer this type of soil thrive here, including species that are not often found elsewhere in Georgia. Many people consider it to be the best wildflower walk in the state from mid-March to mid-April. So many wildflower lovers have visited that a boardwalk was built to protect the plants from being trampled. This has indeed helped, so please stay on the boardwalk.

The Walk From the parking area, walk south along a gravel path between the woods and a planted field to a bridge across Pocket Branch, where a marker commemorates the Shirley Miller Wildflower Trail. Across the bridge, the boardwalk traverses a

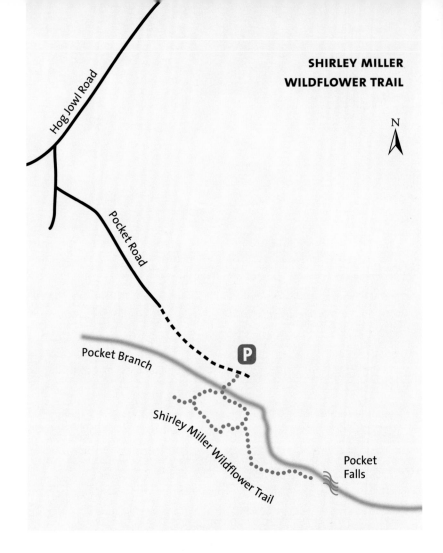

N

loop around the cove floor. Begin the loop to the right, which in early spring passes through masses of **bluebells** mixed with **celandine-poppies**. During the peak many species flower on the slopes to the right of the boardwalk. **Dutchman's-breeches, squirrel-corn, Carolina spring-beauty, toothwort, cutleaf toothwort, rue-anemone, blue phlox,** and **American trout-lilies** are joined by trilliums galore: **decumbent trillium, bent trillium,** and **sweet Betsy.** The **American trout-lilies** (*Erythronium*

Bluebells
(*Mertensia virginica*)

Clusters of pink buds open into blue funnel-shaped flowers that dangle from the tips of arching stems. The leaves are smooth, oval, and gray-green in color; the basal leaves are larger than the stem leaves. In Georgia, bluebells occur rarely, and only in the calcium-rich soils of the northwest, forming patches along streams and in moist areas.

Although many "bluebells" belong to the bellflower family, this one belongs to the borage family, characterized by coiled flower clusters that unfurl and straighten as the flowers mature. *Mertensias* are a wide-ranging genus that have similar clusters of blue or pink flowers. One species can be seen covering moist slopes in the Rocky Mountains, even up into the alpine tundra, where it is dwarfed. Another species grows prostrate on beaches and seaside barrens from Newfoundland to Massachusetts.

americanum) here are unusual because most trout-lilies in Georgia are a different species, *Erythronium umbilicatum*. As you near the farthest point from the entrance, look for **Ohio buckeye**. This is one of the few places it grows in Georgia. The leaves, twigs, and flowers have an unpleasant odor when crushed, so this understory tree is also called fetid buckeye.

As the boardwalk curves back toward Pocket Branch, steps descend to a trail that follows the branch upstream to a waterfall. Footing on the trail is tricky, but the flowers along the way are magnificent at their peak. About 100 yards up the stream, look for the tiny snowflake flowers of **miterwort** among the rocks bordering the stream. Beside the path are **harbinger-of-spring, foamflower, giant chickweed, blue cohosh, wild geranium, perfoliate bellwort, wild oats, white baneberry, sharp-lobed**

Decumbent trillium (*Trillium decumbens*)

The three mottled leaves of decumbent trillium appear to spring directly out of the ground, because its short red stem lies flat and is usually covered by forest litter. This decumbent stem distinguishes it from many similar trilliums with mottled leaves. The stalkless flower, with three narrow maroon petals, rises directly above the leaves. The petals stand upright, while the three sepals are much shorter and lie flat against the leaves.

The genus *Trillium* is divided into two subgenera. The toadshades, like decumbent trillium, have mottled leaves and a stalkless flower. The wake robins have green, unmottled leaves and flowers held above the leaves on stalks.

Although Georgia has more than twenty species of trillium, decumbent trillium is one of the rarer species. It occurs primarily in northwest Georgia, central Alabama, and southeastern Tennessee, usually in rich woods with neutral or basic soils.

liverleaf, and **Canada violet**, along with many flowers you will have already seen on the boardwalk. **Bent trillium** puts on a special display on the slopes above the path. Closer to the waterfall, **woods stonecrop**, **fernleaf phacelia**, and **wild columbine** grow on and around the rocks at the end of the path.

Return by the same path to the boardwalk and continue around to the bridge. Along this last section look for **pennywort**, **yellow violet**, **long-spurred violet**, and **wild hyacinth**.

This is a walk to savor. Stop, observe, and search among the plants for more species we have not listed. Enjoy what may be the best display of wildflowers in Georgia! 🍁

Bent trillium
(*Trillium flexipes*)

This handsome plant has three large, broad, solid green leaves on a long stem. Because its flower stands on a stalk above the leaves, the bent trillium belongs to the subgenus of wake robins. With three broad, creamy white petals, six white stamens, and a white or pale pink ovary, the flower appears nearly white throughout. The flower stalk flexes where it joins the flower, causing the flower to face to one side.

Although it occurs from New York to Minnesota and south to Tennessee and Missouri, the range of this trillium barely dips into Georgia. Here it occurs only at about twenty sites in rich moist bottomlands and woodlands over limestone bedrock. In favored sites it forms large colonies.

Wild hyacinth
(*Camassia scilloides*)

With many six-petaled pale blue flowers on a stalk up to two feet tall, wild hyacinth is a delight found in damper areas along the trail. The flower stalk rises from a clump of grasslike leaves. One of the many calcium-loving plants found in this cove, wild hyacinth is the only member of the genus *Camassia* found in the eastern states.

A relative, common camas (*Camassia quamash*), was prized for its edible bulb by Native Americans and early Euro-American settlers of the plains, as well as by members of the Lewis and Clark expedition. It even sparked a clash between settlers and a party of Bannock and Paiute Indians on Camus ▶▶

Prairie near Fort Boise, Utah, in 1878. Hogs introduced by the settlers were digging up the camas roots, which by treaty the tribes had the right to dig. Troops called in from Fort Boise forcibly settled the dispute in favor of the settlers.

Death camas (*Stenanthium elegans*) has a poisonous bulb that is so similar to that of common camas that many people died from eating it. It can be distinguished from common camas only when in flower.

Celandine-poppy (*Stylophorum diphyllum*)

The species name *diphyllum*, meaning "two leaved," refers to the single pair of deeply lobed leaves on the stem. Other similar leaves are found at the base of the stem. Each stem has one or a small cluster of large, bright yellow flowers. The juice of the plant is also yellow. Some celandine-poppies can be found on the cove floor among the bluebells, but more appear in the slightly higher and drier areas at the base of the bluffs.

The common name celandine refers to *Celandine major*, a Eurasian member of the poppy family with similar yellow flowers. According to Dioscorides, a Greek physician and herbalist of the first century AD, this plant may have been named celandine, which means "of the swallow," because it blooms at the time the swallows return in the spring or because swallows reportedly used the juice to cure blindness in their nestlings.

2
Cedar Glade Walks
Chickamauga National Battlefield Park

...vering Season	March through October
...ak Flowering	April
Walk Length	Six short walks totaling less than 1 mile
Walk Rating	Easy
Restrooms	At Visitor Center
Fee	None

Directions From Fort Oglethorpe drive south on LaFayette Road, which soon enters Chickamauga Battlefield Park. Stop at the Visitor Center for a map.

Environment The Civil War battlefields of Chickamauga and Chattanooga formed the nation's first national military park, created by Congress in 1890. One of the great side benefits of the preservation of these sites has been the protection of a number of cedar glades scattered throughout the park. Cedar glades are openings in the forest where soils over limestone bedrock are so shallow that hardwood trees cannot grow. Only **eastern redcedars** can survive these conditions, and even those seem stunted. There are few shrubs, but many unusual herbs. In fact, several are endemic to this type of glade: **least glade cress**, **purple-tassels**, **Nashville breadroot**, **glade St. John's-wort**, **Great Plains ladies'-tresses**, and **Eggleston's violet**. The wildflowers here tend to appear singly or in small groups rather than in profusion.

The cedar glade habitat is a harsh one for plants. In some places soil is nonexistent. When it rains, the water puddles and then quickly dries up. On a sunny summer day, the rocks and thin soil become very hot. Many of the plants have adapted to this environment by having dissected leaves or many hairs or both—features that reduce heat gain and slow evaporation.

Like desert plants, they tend to bloom profusely in years with adequate rainfall at the right times, but sparsely or not at all in drier years. The conditions may be uncomfortable for walkers, too, on a warm sunny afternoon.

Cedar glades, uncommon in Georgia, are well developed only in the Chickamauga Valley on north–south trending terraces of Chickamauga limestone. The glades in the Chickamauga Battlefield Park are disjunct from the more common cedar glades of the Central Basin of Tennessee, though similar cedar glade

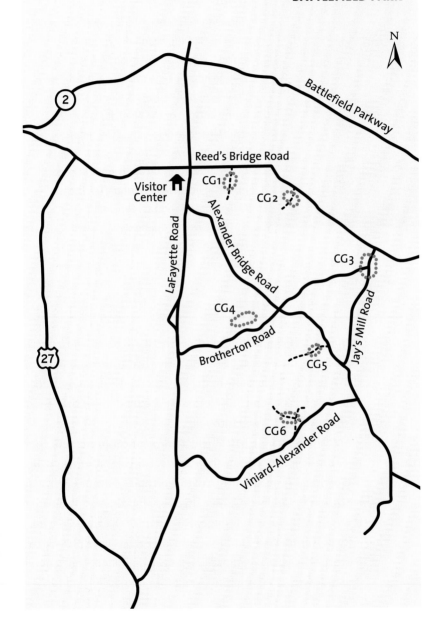

CEDAR GLADE WALKS
CHICKAMAUGA NATIONAL
BATTLEFIELD PARK

N

Battlefield Parkway

2

Reed's Bridge Road

Visitor
Center

CG1

CG2

Alexander Bridge Road

LaFayette Road

CG3

Jay's Mill Road

CG4

Brotherton Road

CG5

27

CG6

Viniard-Alexander Road

Purple-tassels
(*Dalea gattingeri*)

Purple-tassels is one of the prairie clovers, members of the bean family. Prairie clovers all have many small flowers packed into a nearly cylindrical head. The flowers of purple-tassels bloom starting at the bottom of the head, forming a purple fringe below the cylinder of unopened flowers. This species of prairie clover grows only on open areas of cedar glades in northwest Georgia, northeast Alabama, and central Tennessee.

The leaves of prairie clovers were boiled and eaten by Native Americans of the western prairies, and the taproots were used in treating a wide variety of ailments.

communities can be found in northern Alabama and eastern Tennessee. These cedar glades differ in their plants and physical characteristics from those in the Missouri and Arkansas Ozarks, where glades occur on hillsides and are better drained than those in the Southeast (Van Horn 1981).

Although these battlefield areas are now preserved, they were disturbed for decades by warfare, cultivation, and grazing. The area was farmed for thirty years before the major Civil War battle in 1863 and was again cultivated after the war. Even after it was made a national military park, part of the area was a military post from 1898 until 1945, and large tracts were planted for pasture. The post accommodated more than 8,000 horses and mules, as well as 71,000 men (Van Horn 1981).

Least glade cress (*Leavenworthia exigua* var. *exigua*) This tiny annual plant is hard to see even when in flower. Its seed germinates in the fall in the gravelly soil of the glades, and the plant overwinters as a rosette of tiny leaves. In spring new leaves grow to a length of only 2 to 3 inches. They are deeply cut into as many as eleven lobes, with the end lobe by far the largest. Each flower, borne on a leafless stalk, has four white petals notched on the ends and tinged with yellow at the base. The flowers open and close each day, opening most fully on warm sunny afternoons.

The Walks   Here are detailed directions to six of the scattered cedar glade sites, which are not marked on park maps.

Cedar Glade 1: From the Visitor Center go north to the intersection of LaFayette Road and Reed's Bridge Road. Go right (east) on Reed's Bridge Road for 0.3 mile. There is a parking space on the right (south) side of the road from which a trail leads south. The first 100 yards of the trail traverse a cedar glade. In summer, **purple-tassels, glade St. John's-wort,** and **corn-salad** bloom here.

Cedar Glade 2: Continue east an additional 0.5 mile on Reed's Bridge Road to the next parking space on the right (south) side of the road. Follow the trail south about 200 yards to where it crosses a trail parallel to Reed's Bridge Road. This glade extends about 20 yards on the left and about 200 yards on the right. **Thimble-weed, blazing star, rattlesnake-master, coneflower,** and **mountain-mint** flower in summer in this glade.

Nashville breadroot (*Pediomelum subacaule*, synonym *Psoralea subacaulis*)

Nashville breadroot is found in dry, gravelly prairielike openings in northwest Georgia, Tennessee, and northern Alabama. Its blue or purple flowers grow in short, thick racemes on hairy stalks. The leaves, palmately divided into five to seven parts, also have hairy stalks. Each flower produces a pod with a single seed.

In the same genus is Indian breadroot (*Pediomelum esculentum*), which the tribes of the Great Plains used as a vegetable, often storing the root for winter use.

Cedar Glade 3: To find this glade, continue east on Reed's Bridge Road for about 0.9 mile to Jay's Mill Road. Turn right (south) and go 0.2 mile to a parking area on the right. The road system separates the glade into two parts. One part is along the east side of Jay's Mill Road across the road from the parking spot. The other part lies on the southwest corner of the junction of Brotherton Road with Jay's Mill Road. In spring hundreds of **Nashville breadroot** lift racemes of deep blue flowers above the gravelly soil. If the season has been too dry, other plants may dominate: **southern ragwort**, **nettle-leaved sage**, **lyre-leaved sage**, **common cinquefoil**, and **hairy phlox**.

Cedar Glade 4: Drive south on Brotherton Road 1.3 miles from the junction with Jay's Mill Road to a parking space on the right. About 90 yards farther south on the road there is a grassy path to the right, opposite an information sign for Hazen's Brigade no. 10.

Great Plains ladies'-tresses
(*Spiranthes magnicamporum*)

Ladies'-tresses, members of the orchid family, have numerous white, greenish, or yellowish flowers in a spiral arrangement on a slender stalk. The green bracts curving around the bases of the flowers resemble a braid. The flowers, white with a yellow coloration on the lowest petal, appear in October. By flowering time, any leaves at the base of the stem have withered or disappeared. Although there are many species of ladies'-tresses, this is the only one with a yellow center and no basal leaves that flowers on the cedar glades this late in the year.

Great Plains ladies'-tresses are found in Georgia only in the Ridge and Valley province of the northwestern corner, but occur from there westward into the midwestern prairies.

Lime stonecrop
(*Sedum pulchellum*)

Stonecrops are named for the rocky places where they prefer to grow, in shallow soil that accumulates on or in the cracks of the limestone of cedar glades. Their fleshy leaves and stems help them store the water that quickly drains from the stony soil. Their flowering stems can be as tall as 18 inches with many narrow rod-shaped leaves. The delicate flowers of rose pink to white crowd along a whorl of short horizontal branches at the top of the stem.

The cedar glade is about 170 yards down the path and extends about 150 yards to the left and 200 yards to the right of the path. This one is a real gem. In spring the endemic **Eggleston's violet, hoary puccoon, hairy phlox,** and **Nashville breadroot** all bloom. Summer brings **corn-salad, glade wild-petunia,** and **glade St. John's-wort,** and in fall **Great Plains ladies'-tresses** flower.

Cedar Glade 5: Turn around and go back to Alexander's Bridge Road, turn right, and continue on Alexander's Bridge Road for 0.6 mile. Parking spaces are on both sides of the road. Park on the right, and take the horse and hiking trail to the right of the road. This glade is 620 yards down the trail. This wide open, rocky area seems greatly disturbed by horses and other activity, but a search, especially around the edges, reveals wonderful plants. In early spring look for the tiny four-petaled white blossoms of **least glade cress,** which is easy to miss. **Hoary puccoon, lime-barren sandwort,** and **Nashville breadroot** will be more visible. In late spring **lime stonecrop, purple-tassels, Nashville breadroot,** and **spider milkweed** all flower, while **glade St. John's-wort, sundrops,** and **mountain-mint** bloom in summer.

Cedar Glade 6: The last glade is 1.3 miles from the Cedar Glade 5 parking spot. Continue south on Alexander's Bridge Road to Viniard–Alexander Road. Turn right (west) and drive to the second trailhead on the right. Parking is on the left. At the beginning of the trail, look left for a low, moss-covered rock shelf, where **lime stonecrop** blooms in summer. The trail opens into the large cedar glade, which is colorful in spring with **purple-tassels,** the blue of **Nashville breadroot,** and the yellow of **tall coreopsis.** In early summer **coneflower** blooms.

3
Keown Falls Trail
Chattahoochee National Forest

Flowering Season	April through October
Peak Flowering	April and May
Walk Length	1.8 mile loop
Walk Rating	Moderate difficulty with elevation gain of 415 feet
Restrooms	At parking area
Fee	Parking fee

Directions
From Villanow drive east on Ga. 136 for 0.4 mile. Turn right (south) on Pocket Road. Drive nearly 5.5 miles to gravel road on right. The Keown Falls parking area is at the end of the gravel road, about 0.4 mile.

Environment
The walk begins and ends in a hardwood forest with **oak, hickory, American beech, sourwood**, and **tuliptrees**. The right (north) part of the loop follows a creek through a moist hardwood cove before switchbacking up the slope to the waterfall (which may be dry in summer). The trail passes behind the falls and continues just below sandstone and shale cliffs for about 0.2 mile. Then it passes a second falls before descending through a dry hardwood forest to return to the beginning of the loop.

The Walk
In early spring numerous wildflowers bloom along the path to the falls. They include **giant chickweed, violet wood-sorrel, pussy-toes, wild geranium, bluets, common blue violet, toothwort, tiny anemone, perfoliate bellwort, bird-foot violet**, and **early saxifrage**. In the wetter areas, **sweet-shrub** sports spice-scented maroon flowers, while in the drier area, where the trail switchbacks up the slope, **pinxter-bloom** is covered with fragrant pink blossoms before its leaves come out.

Later in spring many more species come into bloom. More than half are in the lower forest before the stream crossing and the slope to the waterfall: **Catesby's trillium**, the perky **wild geranium, slender blue-eyed-grass, lyre-leaved sage, yellow wood-sorrel, Solomon's-plume, giant chickweed, dwarf cinquefoil, sweet-shrub, wild yam, maple-leaved arrowwood, blue-star, whorled horse-balm, meadow-parsnip, Solomon's-seal**, and even **poison ivy** (yes, it does have a cluster of white flowers, but you wouldn't want to touch them). Along the switchbacks to the

KEOWN FALLS TRAIL

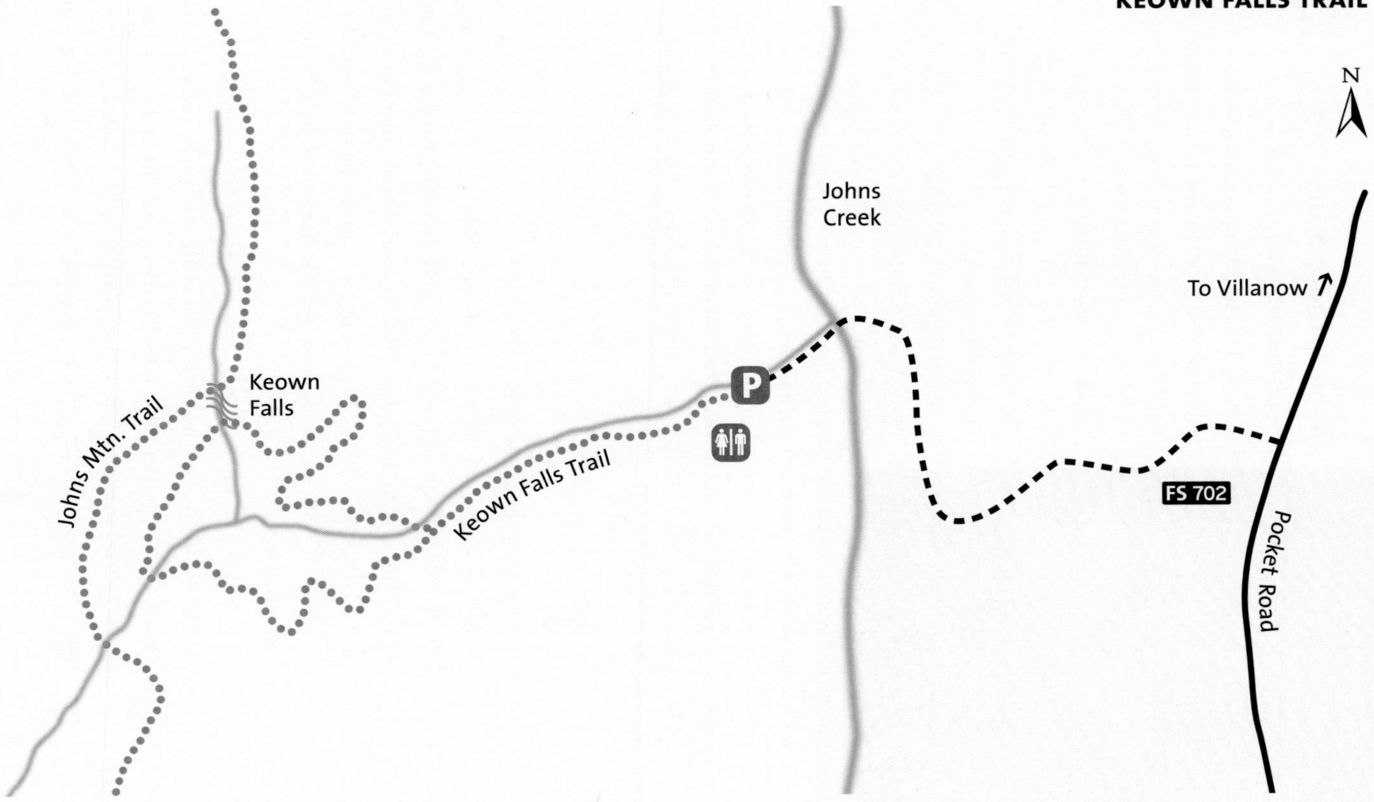

N

To Villanow ↑

Pocket Road

FS 702

Johns Creek

P

Keown Falls Trail

Keown Falls

Johns Mtn. Trail

Whorled horse-balm (*Collinsonia verticillata*)

Whorled horse-balm has unbranched stems up to 2.5 feet tall with two pairs of large, toothy, oval leaves so close together that they appear to be a whorl of four. Numerous flowers in a tall narrow cluster rise above the leaves. Each flower has five purplish petals forming two lips, the lower one fringed.

Peter Collinson, for whom this genus is named, was a cloth merchant in London, with agents overseas. He used his far-flung connections to obtain interesting plants for his garden and those of friends. In North America, John Bartram, a Philadelphia botanist, was his chief collector and wrote of another species of horse-balm, *Collinsonia canadensis*, that it was called horseweed because "horses are very greedy of it [and] it also is good for sore gall'd backs" (Coffey 1993, quoted from Harper 1998).

falls, plants that like drier places hug the slope. Dainty **bluets** border the path, along with **summer bluets** and **rattlesnake-weed**. Also blooming is the little **yellow star-grass**, a member of the amaryllis family. At this time **mountain laurel** puts on a special display. Its white to pink flowers spread through the forest in a magnificent swath. One might take up photography just to capture the scene.

At the top of the trail, the steep stairs to the overlook are worth climbing for the view of the valley and the falls directly below. As you go back down the stairs, turn right on the trail and walk behind the falls. Interesting photographs can be made from this vantage, and the spray is cooling on a warm day. The vine

Yellow star-grass
(*Hypoxis hirsuta*)

True to its name, yellow star-grass sports six-pointed yellow stars on short erect stems emerging from a clump of grasslike leaves. Both leaves and stems are hairy. This diminutive member of the amaryllis family brightens open woods and meadows from Florida into Texas and north to Maine throughout the spring. Several similar species of yellow star-grass grow in the Southeast. Some botanists believe all may actually be a single species.

Turtlehead
(*Chelone glabra*)

It is fitting that a plant called turtlehead is fond of wet sites such as stream banks and wet woods. The white flowers, sometimes tinged with pink or purple at the tips, are two lipped, the upper lip arching over the hairy lower lip. They do resemble turtle heads, but have also been called codhead, fishhead, and snakehead.

The flowers are borne in a spikelike raceme on arching stems up to 5 feet long, with toothed oval leaves. The leaves have a bitter tasting juice and have been used medicinally for a variety of ailments including skin eruptions, liver diseases, and intestinal worms.

that covers the walls behind the falls is **climbing hydrangea**. As the trail continues along the ledge below the bluff, blooms of **Virginia dwarf-dandelion** and **Jack-in-the-pulpit** can be found. The very small greenish-yellow flowers of the **strawberry bush** are not impressive, but in fall the spectacular orange-red fruits give this shrub its other name, hearts-a-burstin'. Soon the trail passes a second waterfall that drops from the cliff top into a ferny grotto. An unusual fern, **mountain spleenwort**, can be found past the second fall on the vertical rock face just after a bend in the trail. From here the trail down the dry slope has fewer flowers and few new species.

Pipsissewa
(*Chimaphila maculata*)

The woody erect branches of pipsissewa grow from underground stems. Their lance-shaped evergreen leaves have white streaks along the midrib and larger veins. Two or three flowers nod on arched stalks from the tops of short stems no taller than 8 inches, but it is worth the effort to get down for a good view of the blossoms. In the center of each is a globular green ovary with a knobby green stigma. The ten surrounding stamens are split in two and arch outward, while the five waxy white petals curve upward. Each flowering stem resembles an ornate lamppost from some earlier era.

Also known as spotted wintergreen, pipsissewa's leaves were used medicinally by Native Americans and as a tea by early settlers. It was also used to flavor root beer.

Indian-pink
(*Spigelia marilandica*)

Indian-pink's eye-catching splashes of bright color are hard to miss. The 1.5-inch tubular flowers are bright red on the outside and yellow within. The tip of the tube splits into five pointed lobes that flare outward, revealing the yellow interior. The flowers are in arching one-sided clusters at the tips of erect stems, the lowest flowers blooming first. Four to seven pairs of large oval leaves with pointed tips are spaced along the stem.

Indian-pink prefers rich, moist woodlands with near-neutral soils. Usually found singly or in small groups, it can form large colonies in favored locations. Its striking flower clusters and true green leaves make it a popular garden plant.

Native Americans first used Indian-pink to treat intestinal worms. By the early 1800s it was so widely used, and even exported to Europe, that it was collected to near extinction. Because the active alkaloids present in the plant often caused severe side effects, people finally quit using it, and wild populations of the plant eventually recovered.

In late spring and early summer the walk through the forest up to the creek crossing features some real beauties. Deep blue **Ohio spiderwort** and red and yellow **Indian-pink** are colorful accents. **White milkweed, summer bluet, flowering spurge**, and **hairy skullcap** also are in flower. On the dry slope up to the falls the white flowers of **pipsissewa** arch downward on short stems. Here, too, is **Appalachian beard-tongue**. Under the falls and along the cliffs, **climbing hydrangea** will be blooming. **Daisy fleabane** will also be blooming at this time along the cliffs, and a shrub, **New Jersey tea**, will have clusters of dainty white flowers in the wetter area by the creek.

In fall **asters** and **goldenrod** flower in profusion. Most are hard to distinguish as to species, but **wreath goldenrod, wood aster**, and **field goldenrod** can easily be identified. The unusual red and orange fruit of the **strawberry bush** can be seen now. **Beech-drops**, a parasitic plant, grows under beech trees, drawing nourishment from their roots. The plant, yellow or purple and without chlorophyll, often grows in bunches under affected trees. **Elephant's-foot** will be everywhere. Around the creek look for the tall stems of **turtlehead** with its curious pinkish-white flowers. It may even have its feet in the water. On the dry slope up to the falls one can find **golden-aster, grass-leaved golden-aster**, and the dainty **southern harebell**. On the cliff walls look for the blooms of **rock alumroot**.

This hardwood forest has beautiful leaf color in the fall, another good reason to visit at this time.

4
Pocket Recreation Area Interpretive Trail
Chattahoochee National Forest

owering Season	April through October
Peak Flowering	April and May
Walk Length	1.1 miles
Walk Rating	Easy, relatively flat
Restrooms	At picnic area parking or at campground, beyond a bridge over the spring
Fee	Parking fee

Directions

From Villanow drive east on Ga. 136 for 0.4 mile. Turn right (south) on Pocket Road and drive about 7 miles, past the entrance to Keown Falls on the right and just past the Pocket Recreation Area campground entrance on the left. The entrance to the Pocket Recreation Area picnic area is also on the left (east) side of the road. Beware of the speed bumps on the entrance drive; they tend to scrape the bottom of low-clearance vehicles even at low speeds. After parking, reach the trailhead by walking along the continuation of the road through the parking area, which is blocked by a gate so cars will not enter. Within 25 yards, you will see a trailhead sign with a map of the trail. Start the trail to your right.

Environment

The interpretive trail loops through a colluvial forest on the floor of a north-facing cove below Horn and Mill Mountains. The white limestone at the base of the cove eroded faster than the sandstone and shale that form the surrounding ridges. Several springs feed the creek that flows out of the cove near the entrance (Pfitzer 1993; Homan 1997). This mesic deciduous forest includes **white oak**, **tuliptree**, **American beech**, and **American hornbeam**. After about 100 yards, the trail reaches an area damaged by the blizzard of 1993 where there

are many downed trees and the canopy is more open. Just beyond this area is a fine example of a limestone sink. Such sinks "are formed by the collapse of the roof of underground caverns dissolved out of solid limestone by subsurface streams and seepages" (Wharton 1978). Farther along, the forest becomes drier and includes pines.

The Walk   Although this is a short trail, there is plenty to see— one spring we counted thirty-seven species in bloom. Many plants flourished in the increased light after the blowdown opened up the canopy.

In early spring the path immediately beyond the trailhead sign is bordered by tiny **bluets** with yellow-centered blue flowers. **Giant chickweed**, which is much prettier and better behaved than the invasive lawn chickweed, **common blue violets**, and **tiny anemone** also greet the walker. Up in the understory, blooms of **red buckeye** and **flowering dogwood** color the forest view. Other early spring flowers along the trail are **violet wood-sorrel**, **dwarf cinquefoil**, **bird-foot violet** (look for leaves shaped like a bird's foot), **pussy-toes**, and **toothwort**. **Trailing arbutus**, a prostrate woody plant, has fresh white to pink flowers contrasting with last year's weather-beaten leaves, because new leaves appear only after flowering.

Later in spring, most of these plants are still blooming, but others appear as well. At the beginning of the trail, the petals of nodding **Catesby's trillium** are white at first, then turn a beautiful rose enlivened by yellow anthers. **Lousewort**, with yellow to maroon flowers and fernlike leaves, **Solomon's-plume**, **wild geranium**, and **meadow parsnip** also welcome the visitor at the beginning of the trail. At the blowdown area are **two-flowered Cynthia** and **foamflower**, with its long-lasting blooms. The large white flower of **mayapple**, with yellow stamens and pistil, is easily missed, because the flower hides below two big maplelike leaves. Under the leaves of **heart-leaf** look for flowers that resemble little

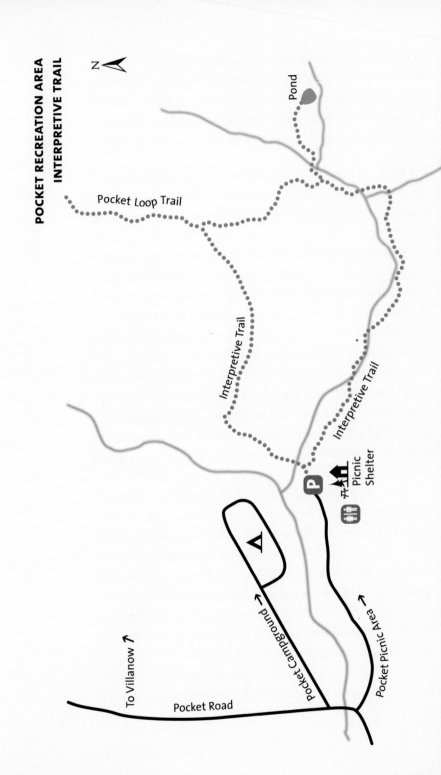

POCKET RECREATION AREA
INTERPRETIVE TRAIL

Pond

Pocket Loop Trail

Interpretive Trail

Interpretive Trail

Picnic Shelter

To Villanow

Pocket Road

Pocket Campground

Pocket Picnic Area

White milkweed
(*Asclepias variegata*)

White milkweed has bright white flowers with purplish centers in compact rounded umbels. Stems are single and unbranched, with four to seven pairs of bright green oval leaves. One to three flower clusters are at the tip of the stem and at the upper leaf nodes. Parts of the plant can be eaten, but only after they are thoroughly washed and boiled to remove the toxic alkaloids in the milky sap.

Milkweeds have a unique flower structure. All flower parts except the pistil are in fives. Outermost is a ring of inconspicuous sepals, curved backward toward the stem. Next come broad petals, united into a short tube at the base. Within the petals, the anthers form another short tube. From inside this tube arise incurving segments, or hoods, to form a corona. From each of the hoods a curving horn points to the pistil at the center of it all.

The masses of pollen on the anthers are attached to sticky glands that may trap insects visiting the pistil. If they are strong enough to pull free, they will carry the pollen clinging to their legs to another flower, but weaker insects may be trapped and die. Pollinated flowers form large seedpods containing hundreds of flattened brown seeds attached to long silky hairs that can float long distances on a breeze. During World War II, this milkweed silk, five times more buoyant than cork, was used to stuff life jackets.

brown jugs. Adding to the display are **wood anemone, golden groundsel, rattlesnake-weed, Solomon's-seal, wild yam** (a low growing vine), and **buttercups**. One of the many photogenic species of spiderwort, **wideleaf spiderwort**, is in the blowdown area

Devil's-bit
(*Chamaelirium luteum*)

An uncommon plant of moist, rich woodlands, devil's-bit stands out when in flower. A tall spike of small, white flowers rises above a rosette of blunt, oval basal leaves. The leaves on the stem are lance shaped and decrease in size from bottom to top. Male and female flowers are on separate plants. Female plants are taller and have leafier stems, but the flowers are less showy than the male's. The male spike curves or droops after all the flowers have opened and may appear yellowish because of the pollen.

The common name comes from a myth that the devil bit into the plant's root to prevent mankind from using its medicinal properties. Another more pleasing name is fairy wand.

too. Pay attention to the shrubs: **painted buckeye, highbush blueberry, maple-leaved arrowwood, deerberry,** and **sweet-shrub** are all in flower at this time.

After the limestone sink, you will enter a pine wood where you can find the relatively rare **pink lady's-slipper** orchid, a state protected plant. Soon a boardwalk crosses spring-fed streams. **Blue-eyed-grass** and **yellow star-grass** can be found here. Beyond is an open area that seems to be recovering from the storm. Here **downy phlox, southern ragwort,** and **toadflax** bloom in spring.

About 20 yards past this meadow the trail meets an old dirt road. A sign directs hikers to the left to return to the beginning of the trail. Most of the flowers along the road you will have already seen.

Spotted touch-me-not (*Impatiens capensis*)

Although it is an annual, growing anew from seed each year, spotted touch-me-not forms large colonies of six-foot-tall plants in moist woods and along stream margins. The stems are fleshy and translucent, with large, oval, toothy leaves on long petioles. The leaves have a whitish water-repellent coating, which causes rain or dewdrops to stand on them, where they catch the sunlight, giving them another common name, jewelweed. The name touch-me-not refers to the ripe seed capsules that split open when touched, flinging their five seeds for long distances. No doubt this helps it spread rapidly over large areas.

The red-orange flowers spotted with deep red or maroon appear from May till frost, dangling on wiry stalks. They are a favorite of hummingbirds.

The juice of the stem and leaves is a well-known treatment for poison ivy and stinging nettle, and has been used for athlete's foot as well.

Late spring and summer bring a new palette to the wild-flower mosaic of this trail. At the beginning, **hairy skullcap**, with its raceme of helmetlike blue flowers, and **white milkweed**, with flowers in a rounded umbel that looks like half a snowball, make a striking contrast. As the trail opens into the blowdown area, one can find **lovage, devil's-bit, whorled loosestrife** with tiny yellow and red starlike flowers in the leaf axils, bright red **fire pink**, and **narrow-leaved skullcap**. The tubular blooms of **Indian-pink** are red outside and yellow within, in an arched cluster. The shrubs include **wild hydrangea, strawberry bush, sweet-shrub**, and **New Jersey tea**. Along the trail between the

Great blue lobelia
(*Lobelia siphilitica*)

Growing to 5 feet tall, its long racemes crowded with inch-long bright blue flowers, this is an impressive plant of moist woods, roadsides, and banks. The five petals form a tube with two lips, the upper divided into two pointed lobes, the lower into three downward-arching lobes marked with white. The outside of the tube is a paler blue with dark blue stripes. A peculiarity of the lobelias is that the stamens form a column around the style, which protrudes through the split in the upper lip and has a tuft of hairs (a beard) at its tip.

The species name *siphilitica* indicates its use as a syphilis cure in the eighteenth century, later found to be ineffective.

Whorled loosestrife
(*Lysimachia quadrifolia*)

Whorled loosestrife is an occasional plant of moist to dry thin woods and openings, as it prefers sunny spots. Whorls of three to six lance-shaped leaves (usually four) are borne on erect stems. Starry five-petaled, yellow flowers are held laterally on long, thin stalks arising from the leaf axils, usually one for each leaf in the whorl. The petals are stained dark red toward the center and may be streaked with black.

European plants of this genus were said to prevent plow oxen from fighting if placed upon their yokes, while American colonists added loosestrife to oxen feed to calm their tempers.

limestone sink and the dirt road, **thick-leaf phlox, flowering spurge, resinous sunflower, whorled-leaf coreopsis, goat's-rue, black-eyed-Susan,** and **Appalachian beard-tongue** can be found. **Venus' looking-glass** appears along the road. Although it grows in many waste places, its flowers are quite beautiful when observed closely.

Return in the fall for a different bouquet. Besides many **asters** and **goldenrods,** look for **small-leaved white snake-root, northern rattlesnake-root, mountain-mint,** and **fireweed,** an eastern plant not related to the much showier western fireweed. Two plants named tobacco can be observed: **rabbit-tobacco,** with small white flowers, and **Indian tobacco,** a blue lobelia with inflated fruit. The tall red stems of **pokeweed** sport clusters of greenish-white flowers, and **spotted touch-me-not** is a bushy green plant with yellow-orange blossoms that look like spotted goldfish hanging on hooks. In the wet areas, **whorled horse-balm, meadow-beauty, golden-aster, cowbane, black-eyed-Susan, great blue lobelia, northern rattlesnake-root,** and **grass-leaved golden-aster** are blooming. And it is hard to miss **heal-all,** a short mint with compact purple flower heads. A naturalized foreigner, it is found throughout the mountains and Piedmont of Georgia.

5
Hidden Pond Trail
Carters Lake
Reregulation Dam Public Use Area

Flowering Season	March through October
Peak Flowering	April and May
Walk Length	0.5 mile loop
Walk Rating	Easy
Restrooms	Portable privies in parking area
Fee	None

Directions

From Resaca drive east on Ga. 136 for 16–17 miles, past its junction with U.S. 411. After crossing U.S. 411, cross the railroad tracks and make the next left turn. Drive about 0.5 mile to the entrance to the first parking area for the Public Use Area. The trailhead is on the right at the edge of the parking area.

Environment

This short trail is near the border between the Great Valley and the Blue Ridge Mountains, the boundary between sedimentary and metamorphic rock. A number of plants preferring calcareous or basic to neutral soils, such as **columbo**, **dwarf larkspur**, **dissected toothwort**, **harbinger-of-spring**, **shooting-star**, and **wild hyacinth** are found at this site, confirming that there is limestone in the bedrock. The loop winds through a hardwood forest, crossing two low hills to reach a beaver pond, and returns along a gravel path lined with **autumn olive** trees and other exotic invasives planted to attract birds.

The Walk

Although this trail was designed for birding, it is also a great place to find botanical gems. Just past the trailhead, take the right fork and cross a bridge. Early in spring, the first flowers are found on the slope just beyond the bridge where **yellow trillium** graces the forest floor. Farther up the hill **dissected toothwort** and **rockcress** can be found. At the top of the second hill, stay left where a trail branches off to the right. The very

earliest flowers, those of the elusive and tiny **harbinger-of-spring**, can be found beyond the observation deck that bridges the creek draining the beaver pond, to the left of the trail where it veers right to border the pond. Although the path circles the pond and may provide good birding, if wildflowers are your priority, we recommend that you stop at the blind and return toward the observation deck. Instead of recrossing the stream, however, turn right along the gravel path bordered with **autumn olive** trees to return to the parking area.

In mid-spring the first slope becomes richer in bloom. **Yellow trillium**, **wild columbine**, **wild geranium**, and **dwarf larkspur** display yellow, red, pink, and white blooms. Each individual larkspur flower looks like a bearded man with a pointed witch's hat. **Mayapple** hides its white flower beneath two large maplelike leaves. On the left look for an **American bladdernut** tree with small clusters of white bell-shaped flowers. Also in flower here is **hairy waterleaf**. After the trail descends the first hill and starts up a second hill, **wild comfrey**, with its soft fuzzy leaves, can be found. The biggest and most spectacular find on this hill,

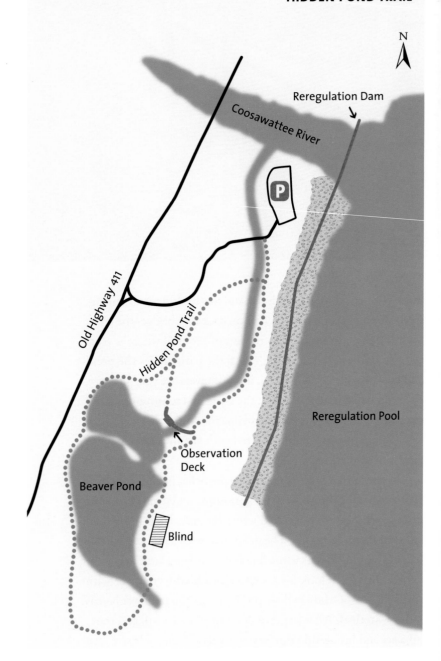

HIDDEN POND TRAIL

N

Reregulation Dam

Coosawattee River

P

Hidden Pond Trail

Observation
Deck

Reregulation Pool

Old Highway 411

Beaver Pond

Blind

Dwarf larkspur
(*Delphinium tricorne*)

Little elfin faces peer out beneath pointed caps as dwarf larkspur sways in the breeze. The uppermost of the five petal-like sepals is elongated into a slightly bent spur, which forms the cap. Pistil, stamens, and four small petals are crowded together in the center of the sepals. The single stem is rarely more than 2 feet tall, much shorter than most other larkspurs. A few deeply dissected or cleft leaves alternate up the stem, topped by a single raceme of purple, blue, or, usually on this trail, white flowers. The seedpods split into three curved sections, accounting for the species name, *tricorne*, or "three horns." All parts of this and other larkspurs should be considered poisonous. Many western species are a grave danger to grazing cattle.

however, is **columbo**, if it is in flower. Some years only the large rosette of basal leaves may be found. Also the delightful **wild hyacinth**, with its pale blue to white flowers, inhabits this area, along with brilliant red **fire pink**. If you see the fallen yellow and maroon flowers of **cross-vine** on the ground, look in the trees overhead for the vine.

After crossing the observation deck and walking to where the path turns right, look at the slope to the left. Low on the slope will be **rue-anemone** and more **dwarf larkspur**, but higher up the white flowers of **shooting-star** dangle from the stems a foot above the rosettes of basal leaves. Here and there will be **southern ragwort**.

In late spring and early summer, on the second hill, tall stems of **black snakeroot** bear racemes of white flowers. Here also is **leatherflower**, a wild clematis vine with leathery, bell-shaped flowers. **Summer bluet** dots the borders of the path. Blooming shrubs along the path include **elderberry** and **silky-cornel**.

In the fall this path yields many **asters** and **goldenrods**, along with **pink eupatorium**, **brown-eyed-Susan**, and **downy lobelia**. In the wet area around the observation deck over the outlet stream are **spotted touch-me-not**, the well-named **turtlehead**, **ironweed**, and **lady's-thumb**. On the path from the bridge to the blind, look for **white snakeroot**. Along the return gravel path, the meadow is colored by white and yellow composites and **purple false-foxglove**.

Shooting-star (*Dodecatheon meadia*)

With stamens pressed together into a narrow cone from which the pistil protrudes, and petals swept sharply back, the flowers do indeed resemble shooting stars, badminton shuttlecocks, or perhaps tiny rockets. The white petals have a maroon ring where they unite at their bases, with a streak of yellow spreading upward into the white, giving the appearance of flames. The flowers hang in a cluster at the top of a leafless stem 6 to 20 inches tall. Smooth, narrow, elliptic leaves form a rosette at the base.

Shooting-star occurs in moist open woodlands and wet meadows, almost always in soils rich in calcium. It is bee pollinated, and as the seeds form, the flower stalk straightens to hold the capsules upright.

Harbinger-of-spring
(*Erigenia bulbosa*)

This dainty plant, only 6 inches high, has lacy leaves and umbels of five-petaled white flowers. Its deep red anthers turn a peppery gray as it ages, so that it is sometimes called pepper-and-salt.

One of the first woodland flowers to bloom, harbinger-of-spring is the prime example of a spring ephemeral. It must get an early start to produce flowers, seed, and store enough nourishment to last until the following spring, all before the deciduous trees leaf out and cut off its sunlight. After this rush of activity, the plant goes dormant, leaving no aboveground parts. Only an underground tuber remains. Harbinger-of-spring may bloom as early as February, and by June it has disappeared.

With such a short active period, it takes many years to reach blooming size. The first year, only a small, undissected leaf appears. Each year thereafter, the single leaf is larger and more dissected. Finally, after six or seven years, the first flowering stem appears, with more appearing as the plant gets older and stronger.

Columbo
(*Frasera caroliniensis*, synonym *Swertia caroliniensis*)

The blooming of a colony of columbo is an impressive woodland event. These bold plants grow 3 to 8 feet tall, with whorls of long, glossy oval leaves at the base and at intervals up the thick, erect stem. The inflorescence, a pyramidal cluster with ▶▶

many flowers, fills the top third of a plant's height. Each individual flower is an inch or more wide, with four or five greenish-white petals spotted with dark reddish brown. Near the base of each petal is a prominent green gland covered with stubby hairs.

Finding columbo in bloom is fortuitous. It flowers only once in its lifetime, after two or more years during which only a clump of large basal leaves can be seen. It takes several years to store enough energy to produce the tall stalk and large flower cluster. After the seeds are formed, the plant dies. In trying to photograph columbo, we found that in some years none of the plants in a population would bloom, but in other years most older plants would.

Yellow trillium (*Trillium luteum*)

With petals and stamens a bright, clear yellow, this is one of the prettiest of the yellow trilliums. The petals are long, tapered, and gracefully curved. The stalkless flower sits directly upon the three broad, strongly mottled leaves.

Yellow trillium prefers rich, mature forests with calcium in the soil. It grows naturally only in northern Georgia, western North Carolina, eastern Tennessee, and a bit of southern Kentucky, but is often confused with yellow forms of other mottled-leaved trilliums. Yellow trillium is distinguished by having no maroon coloration anywhere in the flower.

Because of its beauty and because it spreads into nice colonies, it has often been collected for the garden trade, a practice that has seriously depleted some populations.

6
Tennessee Rock Trail
Black Rock Mountain State Park

Flowering Season	April to October
Peak Flowering	Early May
Walk Length	2.2 mile loop
Walk Rating	Moderate, but with steep sections, including a 440-foot climb
Restrooms	At Visitor Center
Fee	Parking fee

Directions

From Clayton drive north on U.S. 441 to Mountain City. Turn left onto Black Rock Mountain Parkway at the brown sign for the park. Drive up the mountain all the way to the Visitor Center for information and restrooms. Trailhead parking is located about 0.5 mile before the Visitor Center.

Environment

On the southern edge of the Blue Ridge Mountains, along three miles of the Eastern Continental Divide, lies Black Rock Mountain State Park. Georgia's highest state park includes more than 1,500 acres of the top of the divide, with six different peaks over 3,000 feet. It averages more than 80 inches of rainfall per year. Although the park does not have many rare and unusual plants, its diverse habitats support many different species in a relatively small area.

The Walk

Both the Tennessee Rock Trail and the James E. Edmonds Backcountry Trail start from this trailhead. Be sure to stay left on the Tennessee Rock Trail when the backcountry trail diverges to the right shortly after you leave the parking lot.

The beginning of the Tennessee Rock Trail passes through a deciduous forest. In spring **Appalachian** and **perfoliate bellworts** bloom on both sides of the trail. The path zigzags up a steep hillside and turns to the right into a stand of **white oaks**

(the left fork is the end of the trail loop). A search of the herb layer reveals **Catesby's trillium**, **Solomon's-seal**, **sweet Betsy**, and **Solomon's-plume**, all spring bloomers. In autumn look for black fruits hanging from the undersides of the stems of

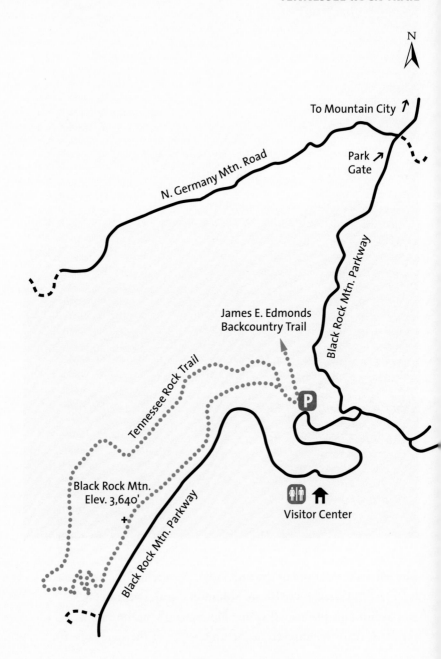

TENNESSEE ROCK TRAIL

N

To Mountain City ↑

N. Germany Mtn. Road

Park Gate ↗

Black Rock Mtn. Parkway

James E. Edmonds
Backcountry Trail

P

Tennessee Rock Trail

Black Rock Mtn.
Elev. 3,640'

Black Rock Mtn. Parkway

Visitor Center

Solomon's-seal and for terminal clusters of red berries on **Solomon's-plume**.

The trail crosses a seep that creates a moist habitat for **red trillium, yellow mandarin, speckled wood-lily**, and **umbrella-leaf**. Along here many **American chestnut** stumps continue to send up sprouts, though within a few years the sprouts will succumb to the chestnut blight that, in the 1930s, virtually wiped out this once-dominant tree in the eastern hardwood forests. Farther along this north-facing slope, **flame azalea** blooms in late spring. In fall **wood aster, southern harebell, wreath goldenrod,** and **white snakeroot** can be seen.

The next stop is a north-facing boulder field just below the summit. Boulder fields were formed above 3,000 feet on the north sides of some of the highest mountains in Georgia during the last glacial period, or Ice Age, of the Pleistocene epoch. Although the

Indian cucumber-root (*Medeola virginiana*)

Though tiny, the flower is a typical lily with three sepals, three petals, and six stamens. The upper whorl of three leaves hides the flowers, while another whorl of five to nine leaves appears about halfway down the single stem. Plants with only one whorl of leaves are either young or weak and usually do not flower. In fall tan leaves stained deep red near the stem contrast with blue-black berries held above the leaves to make this a spectacular plant.

The white tuber of this plant does indeed taste of cucumber and was used by Native Americans as both a food and medicine. Its fanciful scientific name refers to the sorceress Medea, equating the plant's medicinal properties with sorcery.

ice sheets never reached as far south as Georgia, the cold climate of that period caused frequent freezing and thawing cycles, creating ice wedges that gradually broke off chunks of the rock, forming huge jumbles of boulders. See a fine example of this habitat, with wonderful moss-covered rocks, by taking a short side trail to a fenced viewing area. In spring look for masses of **Canada violet** and **mayapple**, as well as **umbrella-leaf**, **blue cohosh**, and **Virginia spiderwort**. In late summer and fall in this area, **monkshood**, **rock alumroot**, **American bugbane**, and **black snakeroot** can be found in flower.

Continuing around the north side of the mountain, the trail passes a scattering of **Indian cucumber-root**, a small lily with greenish yellow flowers hanging below its top three leaves. Keep a close eye along this part of the trail in spring for **showy orchid** sheltered near the base of trees. There are many ferns in this area, but the most handsome in spring is **cinnamon fern**, with tall, rust-colored fertile fronds.

The trail makes a sharp left and connects up with an old dirt road, which it follows for about 0.5 mile. Along this path in spring are more **speckled wood-lilies**. In fall look for **Appalachian gentian** and **stiff gentian**. The trail now enters an area of about 25 acres dominated by **eastern white pines**. After the park was established, the pines, a pioneer species, seeded naturally into an area that had been extensively logged earlier. Not many wildflowers grow beneath the pines, but look carefully in spring for **pink lady's-slippers**, designated a protected plant of Georgia because of the threat from collectors digging it up in the wild. These transplants almost never survive long because they need a mycorrhizal fungus that is rarely present in the soil of their new site. **Pipsissewa** and masses of **Indian cucumber-root** also bloom under the pines in spring.

The trail continues up to the summit and along the crest for about 0.5 mile. This section is more open and tends to have more summer wildflowers. Along the crest, **Carolina lily** may be seen

Speckled wood-lily (*Clintonia umbellulata*)

Speckled wood-lily packs five to thirty flowers into a compact cluster held on a single stem above a rosette of glossy, dark green leaves. The six white tepals (sepals and petals) are speckled with green and purple, while the berries, which appear later, are black. Another species, corn lily or bluebead lily (*Clintonia borealis*), is rarely seen in Georgia but is more common farther north. It has fewer, greenish yellow flowers, and the berries are bright blue. The young leaves of both species have been used as salad greens.

The genus was named for DeWitt Clinton, who held several elected offices in the state of New York. As canal commissioner, he sponsored the creation of the Erie Canal.

Monkshood (*Aconitum uncinatum*)

The large upper petal, curved in the shape of a helmet or hood, gives monkshood its name. Like many other members of the buttercup family, its leaves are deeply lobed or cleft. Its long, weak vinelike stems sprawl along the ground or upon nearby plants. When we first saw monkshood here several years ago it was limited to one or two small patches, which have since spread across a wide area along the trail and down the slope. Despite its beauty, the plant is quite poisonous, containing potent alkaloids. A close relative, European wolfsbane, was used to poison wolves.

Umbrella-leaf
(*Diphylleia cymosa*)

Umbrella-leaf, a bold and conspicuous plant, is found only in the southeastern Appalachians in wet sites with rich soil. Two large leaves up to 18 inches across make the plant stand out even when not in flower. The leaves are round with large teeth and are cleft in the middle nearly into two parts. Small, white, six-petaled flowers grow in a single cluster held above the leaves and are followed by eye-catching blue fruits on red stalks. The plants eventually form large clumps in the moist places they prefer. There are only two species in this genus, the other occurring in Asia.

in summer. In late summer and fall, this area is at its best, with **black snakeroot**, **virgin's bower**, **wreath goldenrod**, and both **pale** and **spotted touch-me-not** in profusion. There is also an extensive patch of **monkshood**.

This summit ridge is part of the Eastern Continental Divide. A drop of rain falling on the north side takes an amazingly long route, sliding into Wolffork Valley and the Little Tennessee River, then to the Tennessee, Ohio, and Mississippi Rivers, and ultimately to the Gulf of Mexico. A drop of rain on the south or west side of the ridge, however, goes into the Chattooga or Tallulah Rivers, thence into the Savannah, and into the Atlantic Ocean.

Toward the end of the summit ridge, steps climb to a rocky outcrop of biotite gneiss where there are marvelous views to the north and south and a number of new plants to be found. In early spring, **serviceberry** flowers on the slopes. In late spring, **mountain laurel** and **mountain rosebay** bloom. In fall look for the yellow blossoms of **witch-hazel**. All year **rockcap fern** clothes the rocks. But beware of the rampant **poison ivy** at the southern view lookout.

As you descend through the deciduous forest back toward the beginning of the trail, note the leaves of **bloodroot**, which flowers in early spring. One of the spring high points along this section is the abundance of **Vasey's trillium** in flower. This large trillium has a whorl of three leaves, each nearly the size of a dinner plate. The maroon flower hangs in the shadows below the leaves.

Continue down the trail to where it intersects the beginning and return to the trailhead. 🍁

Red trillium
(*Trillium erectum*)

Blooming from early April to May, red trillium is one of the earliest trilliums. It grows from 6 to 20 inches tall. The three diamond-shaped leaves are nearly as broad as they are long. The flower is held on a stiff stalk as much as 4 inches long, which can be erect but is sometimes leaning or even declined to just below the leaves. There is considerable variation in the flower. Petals are 1 to 2 inches long, usually a bright maroon fading to duller purplish brown, but may be white, yellowish, or greenish. Stamens are reddish with yellow pollen, and the purple ovary can be seen in their midst from a side view. A good clue to red trillium's identity is its odor, a "wet dog" smell that attracts the carrion flies that pollinate it. Red trillium is also called stinking Benjamin or stinking Willie. It prefers rich, moist acidic soils, often under hemlocks, mountain laurel, or rhododendrons.

Red trillium is common in the northeastern United States, particularly in the Appalachians, but in Georgia is found only in the Blue Ridge Mountains in four of the northernmost counties.

7
Nature Trail and Becky Branch Falls Trail
Warwoman Dell Picnic Area,
Chattahoochee National Forest

Flowering Season	March through October
Peak Flowering	April and May
Walk Length	Nature Trail, 0.4 mile loop Becky Branch Falls, 0.6 mile round-trip
Walk Rating	Easy, with one moderately steep slope
Restrooms	Chemical toilet by picnic shelter at end of road
Fee	None

Directions From U.S. 441 in Clayton drive east on Warwoman Road for 3 miles to Warwoman Picnic Area. Make a wide right turn into Warwoman Dell Picnic Area to avoid scraping the bottom of your car on the pavement junction. Drive to the end of the gravel road to the wide parking area. The trailhead is at the west end of the parking area.

Environment Warwoman Dell is a colluvial valley with a hemlock–hardwood forest drained by Warwoman Creek. The huge **eastern hemlocks** make this a shady, cool place. The understory is made up of **great laurel** and **dog-hobble** shrubs. Among the other trees in this area is the beautiful spring-flowering **Fraser magnolia**, first found by William Bartram in 1775 around what he called Falling Waters and what is today called Martin Creek Falls—a two-mile walk north from Warwoman Dell past Becky Branch Falls on the Bartram Trail. Bartram did not get to name the plant, however, because Thomas Walter published a description of it first, in 1788, before Bartram was able to publish his *Travels* in 1791 (Harper 1998).

Two other historical notes: just before the Civil War, construction began on a railroad from the Atlantic coast to Ohio passing through Warwoman Dell. Economic difficulties

after the Civil War halted construction, but you can still walk on the roadbed near the picnic area. During the 1930s, Warwoman Dell was a Civilian Conservation Corps (CCC) camp and had trout-holding facilities, the remnants of which can be seen near the trail.

The Walk   The nature trail begins at the west end of the parking area, next to the creek. Follow the creek, crossing over a bridge and continuing along the path to Warwoman Creek Falls. Returning from the waterfall, bear left away from the creek to complete the loop and return to the bridge crossing.

The Becky Branch Falls Trail is a small portion of the Bartram Trail, which is blazed with diamond-shaped yellow markers. Walk toward the entrance along the road through the picnic area for about 200 yards. The trail goes to the left, along Becky Branch, switchbacks up to Warwoman Road, then crosses the road and

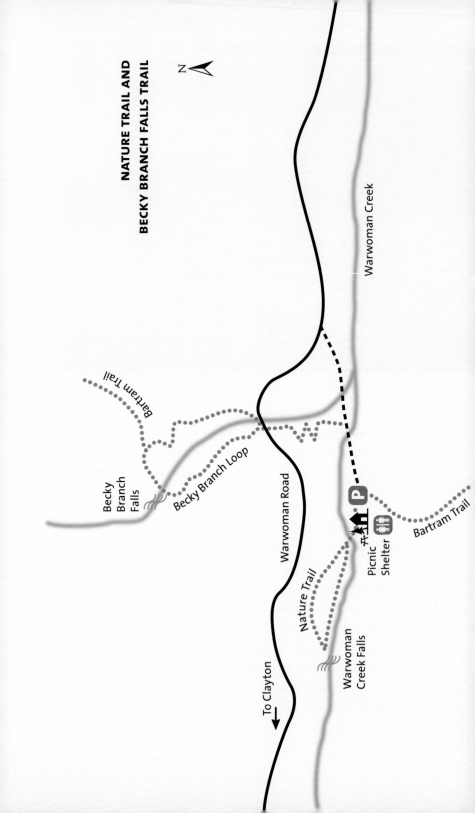

NATURE TRAIL AND
BECKY BRANCH FALLS TRAIL

N

Warwoman Creek

Bartram Trail

Becky Branch
Falls

Becky Branch Loop

Warwoman Road

P

Picnic
Shelter

Bartram Trail

Nature Trail

Warwoman
Creek Falls

To Clayton

Bloodroot
(*Sanguinaria canadensis*)

One of the earliest and showiest of spring wildflowers, bloodroot is also one of the most beloved. Its single flower of eight or more white petals and numerous yellow stamens is up to 1.5 inches across and is borne on a short stem. The single kidney-shaped, irregularly lobed leaf cradles the bud as it emerges from the ground, enlarging after the flower has opened.

The flower stalk and leaf arise separately from an underground rhizome with bright orange-red juice, which gives the plant its common name. Native Americans used the juice as a dye for baskets and clothing and as a decorative stain for face or body. It was used as an insect repellent, rubbed on the skin to attract members of the opposite sex, and ingested as a cough syrup. It contains an active element, sanguinarine, which was used in one brand of toothpaste and mouthwash to prevent plaque and kill mouth bacteria. Its use was discontinued because it caused mouth lesions.

continues up the hill to Becky Branch Falls. After viewing the falls, stay on the Bartram Trail for about another 0.25 mile to a firebreak, just before the trail turns left and begins a continuous descent. Head back toward the falls, but just before you reach it, take the trail that branches off to the left to go down the hill. Cross Warwoman Road and descend to the picnic area by the same trail you came up. For a longer walk, instead of turning around at the firebreak, continue on the Bartram Trail to Martin Creek Falls, 4 miles round-trip from Warwoman Dell Picnic Area.

In mid-March the earliest flowers, **bloodroot** and **spear-**

Jack-in-the-pulpit
(*Arisaema triphyllum*)

With its upright spadix (Jack) covered by a curved flaring spathe (the pulpit), this plant is easily recognized when in flower. Young or weak plants have a single leaf divided into three or five leaflets and do not flower. Older, stronger plants have two leaves, with the flowering stalk between them, and can grow to a height of 30 inches. The tiny flowers are packed onto the spadix. When a plant does not have enough nutrition stored in its underground corm to produce seeds, the spadix has only male flowers. In better years, female flowers form on the lowest part of the spadix and male flowers in the middle. The upper portion has no flowers. The spathe can be striped in two shades of green, or in green and maroon.

Plants with female flowers produce a rounded cluster of bright red fruits. Before long the stem weakens and flops over, resting the fruit cluster on the ground. Chemicals in the red flesh inhibit germination, so that seedlings do not emerge until spring.

Jack-in-the-pulpit, like most members of the arum family, contains sharp calcium oxalate crystals in its leaves, stem, and underground corm, which, if eaten raw, can cause severe swelling. Nevertheless, Native Americans used the corms as a staple food by drying and roasting them.

leaved violet, appear on the nature trail in the picnic area. Very soon they will be joined by Jack-in-the-pulpit, common blue violet, foamflower, and giant chickweed, as well as rue-anemone. Flowers along the trail up to Becky Branch Falls are similar to those on the nature trail, but beyond the falls the trail traverses an area opened up by a forest fire some years ago. In the burned-over area, **trailing arbutus** and **bird-foot violet** bloom in early spring.

Many of these plants continue blooming into mid-spring, especially **foamflower**, which seems to last longer than many other spring wildflowers. In some of the shadiest, wettest areas along the nature trail, very large specimens of **Solomon's-seal, Solomon's-plume, Catesby's trillium**, and **Vasey's trillium** often occur. Other gems along the nature trail are **Indian cucumber-root, white baneberry, hooked buttercup, maple-leaved arrow-wood**, and **strawberry bush**. Look closely for **yellow-root** along the stream after crossing the bridge. Its drooping panicles of tiny maroon flowers are well camouflaged. Where the trail turns away from the creek, **meadow-parsnip** sports bright yellow flat-topped flower clusters. Along the trail away from the creek, look for **showy orchid**.

As you walk along the road toward Becky Branch trailhead, blooms of **crested iris** appear among an invasive exotic plant, **periwinkle**. The Bartram Trail from here up to Becky Branch Falls rewards the walker with some of the same flowers as the nature trail, but on the left side of the falls, clumps of **lady-rue** with delicate white flowers cling to the spray-moistened cliffs. One year we found several huge plants of **Vasey's trillium** just past the falls. In the open burned-over area a totally different group of wildflowers is blooming. Although the young trees here will eventually shade this area, the contrast between the flowers of the mature forest and those that prefer this sunnier, more open area makes the walk particularly gratifying. In this area, look for **yellow mandarin, rattlesnake-weed, sweet-shrub, yellow star-grass, dwarf iris**, and showiest of all, **pinxter-bloom**, a native azalea. **Upland low blueberry** also will be in flower. Notice the many saplings of **tuliptree** and **sassafras**, which are among the first to return after a fire disturbance.

Not much flowers in early summer on the nature trail. The

Dwarf iris (*Iris verna*)

Looking just like a garden iris, except only 6 inches high, dwarf iris spreads by stolons to form large patches in sandy or rocky thin woods. Its very fragrant flower has three erect lavender to violet petals and three downward curving sepals, blue to lavender with an orange streak in the midline. The straight leaves are about 0.5 inches wide and 4–6 inches long.

The similar crested iris is even shorter, no more than 4 inches high, and has broader leaves. Its sepals have a raised, ridged crest of white touched with yellow and bordered by deep violet. Its flower is only slightly fragrant, and it prefers rich mountain coves and forests.

Iris was the goddess of the rainbow, using it as a bridge to travel between heaven and earth. Cultivated irises certainly come in a rainbow of colors. Both of the dwarf irises have become popular as ground cover for native plant gardens.

dominant flowering plant is a shrub, **wild hydrangea**, with clusters of white blooms. The **great laurel** will be just beginning to bloom here and there. **Summer bluets** border the path. **White baneberry** shows clusters of round white fruit, each with a large dark spot that gives it another name, doll's eyes.

If the sunny right-of-way where the Bartram Trail crosses Warwoman Road has not been recently mowed, there may be a charming wild garden of **black snakeroot, thick-leaf phlox, black-eyed-Susan**, and **New Jersey tea**. Along the walk up to Becky Branch Falls, **pipsissewa** blooms, while at the falls, **lady-rue** will still be in flower.

Vasey's trillium (*Trillium vaseyi*)

Vasey's trillium occurs on steep moist slopes of rich mountain coves, where it may spread to form large, open colonies. A spectacular plant, its whorl of three large, rounded leaves can measure more than 20 inches in diameter, while the deep maroon flower with yellow anthers may be 3 inches wide and hangs below the leaves. One of the last trilliums to bloom, its flowers persist till the end of spring.

The genus is called *Trillium* because its parts come in threes or multiples thereof: three leaves, sepals, and petals, and six stamens. Some trilliums have been thought to have aphrodisiac properties and to aid in childbirth.

Once again, the recently burned-over area has a distinct group of plants. Besides **yellow star-grass** and **rattlesnake-weed**, which are still in bloom, **galax, whorled loosestrife, flowering spurge, New Jersey tea, pencil-flower,** white **star-grass,** and **racemed milkwort** can now be found. At the firebreak, where we recommend you stop and return to the parking lot, **white-topped aster** will be blooming.

In the middle of summer **great laurel** brightens the nature trail with its magnificent white blossoms. In the herb layer at the beginning of the trail are **white avens. Lopseed** displays small racemes of tiny white and pink flowers. Elongated spikes of tiny white flowers are those of **jumpseed.** Beware of stinging **wood nettle** along the stream. Uphill from the stream, both **downy rattlesnake-plantain** and **naked-flowered tick-trefoil** are blooming.

Solomon's-plume (*Maianthemum racemosum*, synonym *Smilacena racemosa*)

Because Solomon's-plume is easily confused with Solomon's-seal when the plants are not in flower, it is more commonly called false Solomon's-seal. Both have long arching stems, with elliptic leaves alternating on either side of the stem. However, the tiny flowers of Solomon's-plume are crowded in branched clusters at the tips of the stems, resembling a plume, while those of Solomon's-seal dangle downward at intervals along the stem. The berries that follow the plume of flowers are greenish speckled with red at first, maturing to a translucent red. A common plant of moist deciduous forests, Solomon's-plume spreads by branching underground stems to form large colonies.

Parts of the plant were used by Native Americans as a tonic and a contraceptive, as well as to soothe a crying baby and to treat skin rashes. Settlers used Solomon's-plume as feed for hogs and ponies.

Leaving the nature trail and walking along the road toward the Becky Branch Trail, one is surrounded by blooms of **great laurel**. Climbing the hill to Becky Branch Falls, look closely for **Indian-pipe**, little all-white plants resembling upside-down smoking pipes. **Summer bluets** are still flowering.

The burned-over slope still shows **flowering spurge, pencil-flower, downy rattlesnake-plantain**, and **yellow star-grass**. New blooms include **whorled-leaf coreopsis, yellow false-indigo, angelica, lesser prairie dock, St. Andrew's cross, goldenrod**, and both **smooth** and **winged sumac. Joe-pye-weed, basil bee-**

balm, and **New York aster** grow along the trail as it returns down the hill by Becky Branch.

In late summer to early fall the nature trail has only a few blooms. **Spotted touch-me-not** and **leafy-stemmed elephant's-foot** flower along the stream as you enter the trail at the edge of the parking lot. Elsewhere, **heal-all** and the delightful white **wood aster** greet walkers.

From the road in Warwoman Dell to Becky Branch Falls several new plants are flowering: **cranefly orchid, white horse-mint, northern horse-balm**, and more **wood aster**. Sun lovers in the recently burned area include **leafy hawkweed, golden-rod, asters, spreading sunflower, southern harebell, grass-leaved golden-aster**, and several species of **rosin-weed**. The gem we found on one walk was the curiously named **yellow-fringed orchid**, which is actually quite orange.

This walk is a delight any time of year because of the very pretty small waterfall at the end of the nature trail, and the view of Becky Branch Falls cascading between dense **great laurel** thickets. For a third waterfall, one can walk to Martin Creek Falls, Bartram's Falling Waters, which is a round-trip of 4 miles from the picnic area.

8
Wagon Train Trail
Brasstown Bald Wilderness

Flowering Season	April through October
Peak Flowering	May and September
Walk Length	1.5 miles
Walk Rating	Easy except for rocky footing
Restrooms	In parking area
Fee	Parking fee

Directions

From Blairsville: Drive south 8 miles on U.S. 129/19 to Ga. 180. Turn left (east) on Ga. 180. Drive 7 miles to Ga. 180 Spur. Turn left (north) on the spur, which climbs steeply for 2 miles to the summit parking lot for Brasstown Bald. *From Helen*: Drive north on Ga. 75/17 for 13 miles to Ga. 180. Turn left (west) on Ga. 180. Drive 5 miles to Ga. 180 Spur. Turn right (north) and climb steeply for 2 miles to the summit parking area.

Environment

This walk follows an old roadbed that passes through a forest of northern hardwoods on the north side of Brasstown Bald, which at 4,784 feet is the highest peak in Georgia. Trees include **yellow birch**, **striped maple**, **mountain maple**, **great laurel**, and **mountain rosebay**. At this high elevation, clouds and mists are common. Thriving on all the moisture, old man's beard lichen festoons the large old **yellow birches**. The trail proceeds along rock cliffs, some that provide good views to the west and others, covered with mosses, lichens, and other interesting plants, scenic in and of themselves.

The Walk

From the parking lot, begin on the paved walk to the Visitor Center and observation deck at the summit, which starts between an A-frame building with vending machines and the gift shop. The walk to the summit is 0.5 mile and nearly a 500-foot climb to a magnificent 360-degree view of north

WAGON TRAIN TRAIL

N

Brasstown Bald
Wilderness
Area

Wagon Train Trail

Visitor
Center

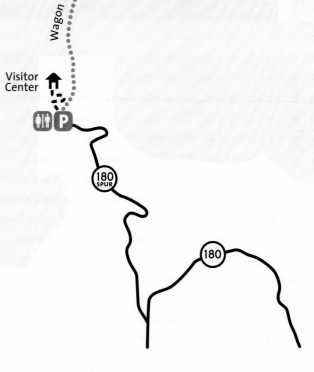

180
SPUR

180

Georgia and parts of three other states. On this particular walk, however, go only about 100 yards up the paved trail to the first unpaved road crossing. This is the Wagon Train Trail, originally meant to be Ga. 66. Turn right onto it. Soon you will pass a barrier in the road and an information kiosk that indicates you are entering the Brasstown Bald Wilderness Area. As the trail continues through the forest, the terrain slopes to the right at first. Then, narrowing a bit, the trail crosses the ridgeline, and the terrain slopes left, with cliffs (actually old road cuts) on the right. Continue to the end of the cliffs, where there are expansive views of ridges to the west. Beyond this the trail actually continues another 5 miles to Young Harris, emerging in a parking lot on the campus of Young Harris College. But our wildflower walk ends here; turn around and follow the same path back to the parking area.

Because of the high elevation, spring comes late to this area. The earliest flowers bloom in late April and early May. **Trailing arbutus** appears on the grassy slope beside the summit trail, just before the turn onto the Wagon Train Trail. After turning right onto the trail, start looking for two small flowers low to the ground: **bluets** and **dwarf cinquefoil**. One of the great sights in early spring is **serviceberry**, whose airy clusters of small white five-petaled flowers brighten the understory before the deciduous trees leaf out. After passing into the wilderness area, look for **red trillium, common blue violet, sweet white violet,** and **tooth-wort**. Although **dimpled trout-lily** blooms at West Palisades and Panther Creek in early March, here it waits until late April or early May. Other early spring bloomers include **Carolina spring-beauty** and **wood anemone**, as well as the **Canada-mayflower**, which looks like a dwarf two-leaved **Solomon's-plume**.

By mid-spring look for another trillium, **Catesby's tril-lium**, along with **cow-wheat, mayapple, false bugbane,** and

Foamflower
(*Tiarella cordifolia*)
Showy racemes of tiny white to pinkish flowers top 6-inch stems. Ten yellow stamens protrude from each flower, giving the raceme a frothy, foamy look. Attractive hairy leaves, lobed like a maple leaf, form a basal rosette. Foamflowers are favorite plants for the woodland garden.

Two variations occur in Georgia, one spreading by underground stems to form large patches, the other simply multiplying into clumps over time. The small seed capsules, whitish and somewhat scooped, remain on the stems long after flowering, making the plant appear to still be in bloom.

Canada-mayflower (*Maianthemum canadense*)

Spreading by branched underground stems, Canada-mayflower forms a ground cover in rich mountain forests. Its flower parts come in twos and fours: each tiny white flower has two petals, two petal-like sepals, and four stamens. The flowers form clusters at the end of short, zigzag stems with two or three oval leaves. The fruit is a berry, green at first, then spotted with red, and finally all red. It is a favorite food of the ruffed grouse.

Canada-mayflower grows in Georgia only at high elevations in the mountains. From there it ranges northward as far as Newfoundland. It is sometimes called false lily-of-the-valley but more closely resembles Solomon's-plume, though in miniature.

Bee-balm (*Monarda didyma*)

Bee-balm is a member of the mint family, with typical square stems and opposite leaves. Tubular bright red flowers blossom in dense clusters or heads at the tops of tall stems and branches, the outermost flowers opening first. Rarely, a second cluster forms a few inches above the first. Below the flower cluster is a ring of bristly bracts inside another ring of several purplish leaflike bracts.

Bee-balm occurs naturally on wooded stream banks in the mountains from ▸▸

Georgia northward to New York. It makes a dramatic garden flower and has sometimes escaped from cultivation and become naturalized elsewhere. Hummingbirds, butterflies, and bees are attracted to its red floral tubes.

Also known as Oswego tea, bee-balm leaves were used by the Oswego Indians of upper New York state to make an aromatic tea, and settlers adopted the custom, particularly after the Boston Tea Party made tea substitutes popular.

Mountain saxifrage (*Saxifraga michauxii*)

The leaves of mountain saxifrage are oval to oblong, coarsely toothed, and widest near the tip, forming a basal rosette. The five-petaled white flowers are in airy loose panicles on stems up to 18 inches tall. This species differs from other saxifrages in that its petals are of unequal size. The three upper ones are larger and have two yellow spots near the base, while the two lower ones are smaller, unmarked, and somewhat spoon shaped. Mountain saxifrage is endemic to the southern Appalachians. *Saxifraga* means "rock breaker" and refers to the habit of plants in this genus to grow in the crevices of rock cliffs.

Botanist André Michaux, for whom this species is named, came to North America under royal sponsorship in 1785 to collect plants for the Jardin des Plantes in Paris. In the next ten years he and his son Francois André traveled through much of the eastern part of the continent and persevered in spite of the French Revolution, loss of support, and even shipwreck to get the plant specimens to France and to prepare publications about them.

Hedge-nettle
(*Stachys tenuifolia* var. *tenuifolia*)

Hedge-nettles are not really nettles and have no stinging hairs, but some do have toothed oval leaves like true nettles. The square stems of hedge-nettles are a clue that they belong to the mint family. *Stachys tenuifolia*, the species found here, grows to 3 feet and has variable leaves, narrow and linear on some plants to narrowly oval on others. It is a common plant of moist woodlands.

The flowers are in a spike at the tip of the stem, with leafy bracts between the flowers. *Stachys* is Greek for a spike or an ear of wheat. Each flower is two-lipped, with the upper lip arching over the stamens. The lower lip is broader and divided into two lateral lobes and a larger middle lobe. The insides of the petals are white streaked with purple, very pretty close-up.

foamflower. Besides scanning for herbs on the forest floor, look upward for the white bells of the **common silverbell** tree, as well as the reddish pink flowers of the high elevation **minnie-bush** and the white flowers of **black chokeberry**, both shrubs. Clusters of pentagonal flowers will be starting to open on the **mountain laurels.** Fresh conelike flowers of the parasitic **squaw-root** emerge from the ground, while **mountain saxifrage** clings to crevices in the cliffs.

In summer **great laurel, mountain laurel,** and **flame azalea** all bloom. A nice surprise near the wilderness kiosk is **swamp azalea,** which grows on moist shrub balds as well as in swamps. The herb layer now has taller plants with brighter colors: the yellow of **sundrops,** the blue of **hairy skullcap** and **wideleaf spider-**

wort, and the greenish white of **poke milkweed**. Tall stands of crimson **bee-balm** wave in the breezes, along with another member of the mint family, **hedge-nettle**, with pink and white blossoms. White flowers include **goat's-beard** and **false bugbane**. Also look for a yellow-flowering bean, **thermopsis**. At the viewpoint at the end of the cliffs where you turn around for the return trip, a short **bushy St. John's-wort** hugs the ground on the rocky roadway.

Fall blooms include **asters**, such as **wood aster**, **heart-leaved aster**, and **many-flowered aster**. In scientific nomenclature they are not asters anymore: because they differ technically from European asters, they have been removed from the genus *Aster* and given new names. **White goldenrod** is here, along with other yellow **goldenrods**. Other fall plants in bloom include **thick-leaf phlox**, **angelica**, and masses of **white snakeroot**. **Mountain saxifrage** and **rock alumroot** cling to the cliffs toward the end of the walk.

The delayed spring bloom schedule at this elevation makes it possible to find spring flowers here after they have disappeared from lower elevations. In summer this trail can be a cool refuge on a hot day, and in fall the deciduous hardwoods display their striking colors while the last wildflowers bloom.

9
Sosebee Cove Trail
Chattahoochee National Forest

Flowering Season	March to September
Peak Flowering	April and May
Walk Length	A total of 0.4 to 0.5 mile, consisting of a loop trail 0.2 mile in length with a 0.1 mile connecting trail through the middle of the loop, forming two loops
Walk Rating	Easy, but be careful on the steep stairs from the road to the beginning of the walk
Restrooms	None. The closest public restrooms are in Vogel State Park.
Fee	None

Directions

From Blairsville: Drive south on U.S. 129. Ga. 180 comes in from the left after 8 miles and is coincident with Ga. 129 until it turns right (west) 1.5 miles later. Turn right on Ga. 180 and drive 3 miles. Parallel parking spaces, enough for about four or five cars, for the cove are on the right. *From Cleveland*: Drive north on U.S. 129 for 22 miles. Pass Turner's Corner, go over Neel's Gap, and just after passing the Vogel State Park entrance on the left, turn left (west) at Ga. 180. Drive for 3 miles to the Sosebee Cove parallel parking spaces on the right side of the road.

Environment

Sosebee Cove is a 175-acre broadleaf deciduous cove forest. Logging of **northern red oaks**, **tuliptrees**, and **American basswoods** in the early 1900s has left a forest of giant old **yellow buckeyes** and young **tuliptrees**. The buckeyes escaped because they were not profitable to log at that time. The one at the first right turn along the trail going clockwise is second in size to the Georgia champion **yellow buckeye**, and not by much. The size of the second-growth **tuliptrees** is also impressive.

The cove faces north below a boulder field that lies above the road. The dark fertile soil contains a lot of humus and retains

moisture even in droughts. Cool north-facing coves provide refuge for plants that once spread farther south when the climate was colder.

Sosebee Cove, said to be a botanist's paradise, is certainly one of the top five wildflower walks in Georgia. It is ideal for a wildflower photographer, because one does not have to lug equipment far to record many beautiful species.

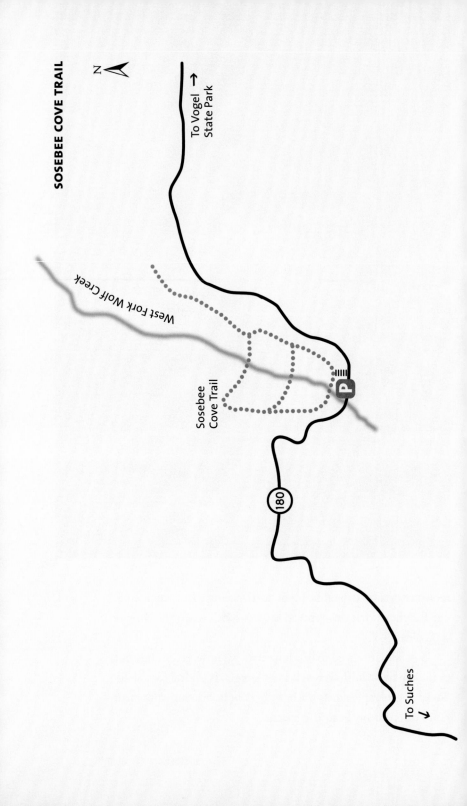

SOSEBEE COVE TRAIL

N

To Vogel State Park →

West Fork Wolf Creek

Sosebee Cove Trail

P

180

To Suches ↓

The Walk   From the parking area, carefully descend the steps to the loop trail. The trail may be walked by starting in either direction around the loop.

Among the first flowers in early spring are **dimpled trout-lily**, **giant chickweed**, and **Virginia spring-beauty**. A prize for the walker this time of year is **Dutchman's-breeches**, with dissected leaves that are as striking in their way as the unusual upside-down-pantaloon configuration of the flower. The sessile flowers of **sweet Betsy**, a common trillium in Georgia, appear too. **Bloodroot**, a member of the poppy family, sometimes cradles the flower in its single distinctive leaf, which lasts long after the flower is gone. **Showy orchid** appears early beside the branch that flows through the center of the cove. Three other plants in bloom will be **Jack-in-the-pulpit**, **blue cohosh**, and **yellow mandarin**.

At least one new species comes into bloom in Sosebee Cove every three or four days from the middle of March through the middle of May (Homan 1997). The blooming sequence varies from year to year, but here is one way it might happen: after the earliest plants discussed above, **toothwort** and **sweet white trillium** are next. In another few weeks, **foamflower, Solomon's-seal, umbrella-leaf**, and **wood anemone** bloom. Toward the end of April come **common blue violet, yellow violet, crested iris, great white trillium, broadleaf waterleaf, Solomon's-plume, mayapple, meadow-rue**, and **perfoliate bellwort**. Early May would add **buttercups, wild geranium**, and **sweet cicely**.

By June the trees leaf out and the spring flowers are in seed. Early July, however, brings the summer blooms: **pale touch-me-not, yellow wood-sorrel**, and **summer bluet**. Later in July, **wood nettle, false hellebore, Turk's-cap lily, Joe-pye-weed, bee-balm**, and **lopseed** flower.

In late summer and early fall come **wood aster, northern horse-balm, white snakeroot, southern harebell, small-**

Dutchman's-breeches
(*Dicentra cucullaria*)

Resembling white pantaloons hanging upside down from an arching clothesline, Dutchman's-breeches bring an unexpected touch of natural whimsy to the spring woodland. The pants legs are formed by long, inflated spurs on the two outer petals. The fragrant flowers are pollinated by bumblebees, which have a proboscis long enough to reach the nectar at the tip of the spurs. Honeybees can reach the pollen but not the nectar.

The compound leaves are deeply dissected, grayish green on top and paler underneath. Dutchman's-breeches is a perennial, growing from a small scaly bulb. It prefers rich woods and north slopes.

Showy orchid
(*Galearis spectabilis*)

Two or more inch-long lavender and white flowers arise on a short stalk from between two glossy oval leaves. In this little orchid, the three sepals and two lateral petals are joined together to form a lavender hood, which arches over the column of fused style and stamens. The third petal hangs downward, and may be all white, or white and lavender, with a long spur extending back from the base and containing nectar at its tip.

Charles Darwin studied European plants of this genus and showed how the arrangement of the flower parts ensures cross-pollination. One species, called long purple, was part of Ophelia's garland. All were used to treat a wide variety of ailments.

Broadleaf waterleaf (*Hydrophyllum canadense*)

The mottled leaves of broadleaf waterleaf are as interesting as the flowers. Broad, lobed, and toothed, in spring they are marked in at least three shades of green to gray, which gives them the splotched, water-marked look from which their name originates.

The flowers are borne on 2-foot-tall leafy stems, in coiled clusters hanging below the topmost leaves. They are bell shaped, with five petals, white or tinged with purple, and united only at the base. The five anthers are on long, elaborately fringed white or lavender filaments.

Broadleaf waterleaf is found in rich, moist cove forests in the mountains of north Georgia and from there north to Vermont and Michigan. In former times it was boiled and eaten as a potherb, and reportedly tastes like parsley.

headed sunflower, woodland sunflower, thick-leaf phlox, Indian tobacco, poke milkweed, whorled loosestrife, and mountain horse-mint.

In fall the fruit of some of the spring plants can be interesting too. The clustered fruit of the **Jack-in-the-pulpit** glows with the brightest red in the woods. **Yellow mandarin** has smooth yellow fruit turning red, **Solomon's-plume** fruit is green turning to red, while that of **Solomon's-seal** is black.

Great white trillium (*Trillium grandiflorum*)

The most spectacular display of spring wildflowers in Georgia's Blue Ridge Mountains is a hillside with thousands of blooming great white trilliums. With large white petals on erect stalks above dark green leaves, they form striking colonies in rich deciduous woodlands.

The three leaves are oval- to diamond-shaped on foot-long stems. The oval petals flare outward and overlap at the base to form a funnel. As they age, they become translucent, with a pink or even rose coloration. The pointed sepals are green, sometimes streaked with maroon. The anthers are long and recurved, covered with yellow pollen.

Deer are fond of trilliums, which must seem to them like deer candy. Overgrazing can cause even large colonies to decline rapidly. Great white trilliums do best in young or maturing forests where some sunlight still reaches the forest floor. The deep shade of mature forests causes decline. Great white trilliums are found from Georgia northward to Canada and west to Minnesota.

Sweet white trillium (*Trillium simile*)

The petals of sweet white trillium are a creamier white and do not curve backward as much as those of great white trillium, so that the stamens and pistil cannot be seen in a side view. Most striking is the dark purple black of the ovary. The flowers are said to smell like green apples. The plants spread to form large clumps but do not usually cover whole hillsides the way great white trillium can. The species name *simile*, meaning similar, is appropriate, since it is similar to and easily confused with several other trilliums.

Although nearly as showy as great white trillium, sweet white trillium is less widely distributed. It is found in only three of the northernmost counties in Georgia, and in the Great Smoky Mountains of eastern Tennessee and western North Carolina.

10
Gahuti Trail
Fort Mountain State Park

Flowering Season	April through October
Peak Flowering	May and June
Walk Length	1.6 miles round-trip
Walk Rating	Moderate, climbs gradually up and over ridges and around coves, with gentle ascents and descents
Restrooms	At office and picnic areas
Fee	Parking fee

Directions *From Chatsworth*: Drive east on Ga. 52 for about 7.5 miles to park entrance on left side of road. *From Ellijay*: Drive west on Ga. 52 for 18 miles to park entrance on right side of road. Steps mark the beginning of the trail on the right side of the park road, not far beyond the entrance. The only parking area for the trail is on the shoulder off the left side of the road at a wide place that has obviously been used by many cars. It may be best to go to the office to turn around and park heading back toward the entrance.

Environment The habitat in this area is a broadleaf deciduous ridge and cove forest. The tops of the mountains in this western part of the Blue Ridge have deeper and richer soils than the ridgetops of the eastern Blue Ridge Mountains, supporting a more abundant herb layer than those farther east.

The Walk This walk, only one short section of an 8.8-mile backcountry loop trail, hugs the tops of the slopes as it skirts a couple of coves, finally descending to the bottom of the second cove to the stream that drains it. In early spring (late April), **flowering dogwoods** create white clouds among the leafless trees of the forest. **Sweet-shrub**'s maroon flowers dot the shrub layer.

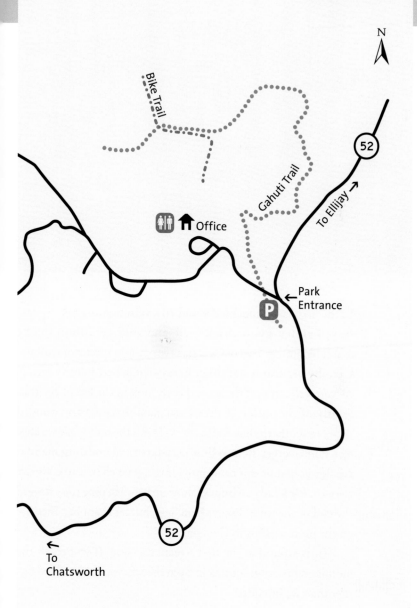

N

Bike Trail

Gahuti Trail

🚻 🏠 Office

To Ellijay →

52

← Park
Entrance

P

52

←
To
Chatsworth

In the herb layer, **speckled wood-lily**, **yellow star-grass**, **spear-leaved violet**, **giant chickweed**, and **wild geranium** can be found blooming. Two of Georgia's twenty-two species of trillium, **Catesby's trillium** and **sweet Betsy**, bloom here in early spring. As you walk around the second cove, look to the left of the trail for **lily-of-the-valley**, an occasional plant that grows on wooded slopes in southern Blue Ridge coves. This is the only place we have seen it in Georgia. Both **yellow mandarin** and **nodding mandarin** flower here at this time, providing a good chance to compare the two. **Pink lady's-slippers** show up beneath pine trees toward the end of the walk. Enjoy them here, but let them be. They are on the protected list in Georgia.

Turn around at the first stream crossing. If you reach the mountain bike trail coming in from the left, you have walked farther than we intended.

By mid-spring more species bloom. Look for a large colony of **bird-foot violet** on the road bank at the beginning of the trail.

Lily-of-the-valley
(*Convallaria majuscula*)

Fat little white bells, emitting a distinctive fragrance, dangle from one side of an arching stem. The two or three narrowly oval pointed leaves are 6 to 12 inches tall, with the flower stalk about half as high. The bases of the leaves sheath the stalk.

This native American lily-of-the-valley forms small open colonies of somewhat scattered plants and is found in wooded mountain coves from Georgia north to Virginia. A Eurasian species, *Convallaria majus*, is widely used as a garden plant and can often be found near old home sites. It has only two leaves, 4 to 8 inches tall, with the flowering stem more than half as tall, often rising above the leaves. It forms dense colonies. The root of both species contains a toxin that affects heart muscle action. The European species has been used as a heart stimulant in small doses.

Pink lady's-slipper
(*Cypripedium acaule*)

Lady's-slippers are probably our best-known native orchids. Their unusual shape has inspired many common names, including moccasin flower and squirrel shoes. *Cypripedium* means Venus slipper.

Pink lady's-slipper rises on a leafless stalk. Its three sepals and the two lateral petals are yellowish green to greenish brown. The larger lower petal is pink veined with red and turned inward to make an inflated pouch, forming the slipper. A narrow leafy bract arches forward ▸▸

over the flower. Rarely, a plant with a white slipper occurs. The two basal leaves are deep green on top and silvery underneath, with prominent veins that give them a ribbed appearance.

In Georgia pink lady's-slipper is found in dry pine woods with acid soil. Farther north it also occurs in bogs. Because people are tempted to dig it up for gardens, it is on the protected list in Georgia. A specific fungus must be present in the soil for the plant to thrive, so these transplants usually do not survive long. The fungus must also be present for the extremely small seed to germinate, and the plant does not reach flowering size for at least seven years. Recent advances in tissue culture may reduce the process by several years, making lady's-slippers available as nursery-propagated plants and reducing pressure on the wild populations.

Wild geranium
(*Geranium maculatum*)

If flowers can be said to have personalities, wild geraniums are cheerleaders. Perky and upbeat, dancing in the breeze, their performance adds color to the spring show. The leaves are divided into five lobes, which are further divided. Those at the base have long stalks, while the single pair on the stem have short stalks. Five-petaled flowers in pink to bright magenta appear in loose clusters of two to five.

The five-parted seed capsule has a thick base and a long pointed beak, leading to another name, cranesbill. When the seed capsule is mature and dry, the five parts of the capsule coil upward from the bottom while still attached at the top, flinging the seeds for some distance. The empty capsules with their five little springs remain on the plant for some time.

Tannin in the root makes it astringent. It has been used to stop bleeding and to treat diarrhea and ulcers.

Nodding mandarin (*Disporum maculatum*, synonym *Prosartes maculata*)

Growing to 3 feet tall with erect branched and forked stems, mandarins look like small shrubs but are actually perennial herbs, dying to ground level each winter. Their alternate leaves are pointed ovals with pronounced parallel veins. Pairs of bell-shaped flowers hang from the ends of the stems, below the last leaf.

The six tepals (sepals and petals) are narrow, tapering to a point, and not joined at the base. The tepals of nodding mandarin are creamy white to pale yellow, flecked with purple. They have pronounced claws or abruptly narrowed segments at their bases, beyond which they flare outward. The anthers are on long filaments that extend well beyond the tepals. Fruit is a hairy red berry.

The similar yellow mandarin has deeper yellow tepals, which taper gradually to their bases and have no markings. Its fruit is a smooth red berry.

Indian-physic presents a bouquet of star-shaped white flowers. The dark maroon flower of **Vasey's trillium** nods below three huge leaves. Many of the common spring wildflowers appear on this trail: **rue-anemone, wood anemone, mayapple, Jack-in-the-pulpit, Solomon's-seal, Solomon's-plume, dwarf cinque-foil**, and the diminutive **cow-wheat**.

By early summer there has been quite a turnover in species. **Summer bluets** line the trail. In the first power line cut, **southeastern beard-tongue** blooms. Farther along the trail are **fire pink, whorled loosestrife, whorled-leaf coreopsis, pipsissewa**, and **Indian-pink, yellow wood-sorrel**, and **hairy skullcap**. By

Fire pink (*Silene virginica*)

Not pink but a pure bright red, fire pink gets its name from its five pinked, or notched, petals. Fire may refer to its fiery red color or to its preference for open disturbed areas such as those created by wildfires. The 1- to 2-inch flowers occur in open clusters on tall stems, with several narrow oval- or lance-shaped leaves at the base and one to four pairs on the stem. Sticky hairs on the sepals of plants in this genus give them another name, catchfly.

now **Solomon's-plume** is already starting to form fruit. Adding to the display are the tall spires of **black snakeroot**, along with **Ohio spiderwort**, **poke milkweed**, **galax**, and **foamflower**. At this time several shrubs will be flowering: **wild hydrangea**, **flame azalea**, and **mountain laurel**.

Fall on this trail brings **white snakeroot**, **pokeweed**, **northern horse-balm**, **thick-leaf phlox**, and **southern harebell** with its delicate candelabrum of tiny blue bells. **Appalachian gentian**, with white-and-blue striped flowers, is found here, but this species, *Gentiana decora*, similar to pale gentian, is not included in most field guides. **Featherbells** has large airy clusters of tiny greenish white flowers. **Wood aster** forms drifts of toothed oval leaves, with open clusters of white-rayed flower heads whose yellow centers turn a dull red with age. Among the many **goldenrods**, look for **wreath goldenrod** with small clusters of yellow flowers at each leaf axil.

11
Panther Creek Trail
Chattahoochee National Forest

Flowering Season	March through October
Peak Flowering	Mid-March through May
Walk Length	7 miles round-trip to waterfall
Walk Rating	Moderate, with one tricky scramble over a rock ledge and a steep descent to the bottom of the falls
Restrooms	At the picnic area
Fee	Parking fee

Directions The turnoff for Panther Creek Recreation Area is about 3 miles north of Hollywood or 3 miles south of Tallulah Falls on U.S. 441 at Glen Hardman Road. Turn west on Glen Hardman Road for 0.1 mile, then turn right (north) on Historic 441 for 1 mile to the parking area on the left (west) side of the road. The trail begins on the east side of the road, opposite the parking lot. Start early and take lunch to enjoy at the waterfall, 3.5 miles down the trail along Panther Creek. Although the trail proceeds for another 2.5 miles, these directions stop at the falls.

Environment This is a ravine and bluff forest of northern affinities, located in the Gainesville Ridges in the Brevard Fault Zone. The dominant trees are **tuliptree**, **eastern hemlock**, **eastern white pine**, **oak**, **hickory**, and **red maple** (Wharton 1978).

The Walk In early spring, **trailing arbutus**, a woody member of the heath family, trails its delicate white or pink blossoms along the slopes near the beginning of the trail. In spring look for **Catesby's**

bridge and just past it, **bedstraw, Carolina cranesbill, yellow wood-sorrel**, and **lyre-leaved sage** bloom in spring. After passing under the bridge and climbing a small incline, the trail crosses a drier area before following the creek again. Here you can see **dwarf irises** in spring.

As the trail rejoins the creek, look for white, bell-shaped flowers on the drooping stems of **dog-hobble** in spring and the arching spires of **devil's-bit** in summer. On the next upward grade, **green-and-gold** forms a low ground cover in early spring, and **heart-leaf, yellow star-grass**, and **rattlesnake-weed** flower later in spring.

The next major stop is an open power line right-of-way where sun-loving plants grow: **bird-foot violet, hairy phlox, southern ragwort**, and on the edges, **trailing arbutus**. Along the next stretch, **great laurel** flowers in summer. These large evergreen shrubs are so dense that little else grows along here.

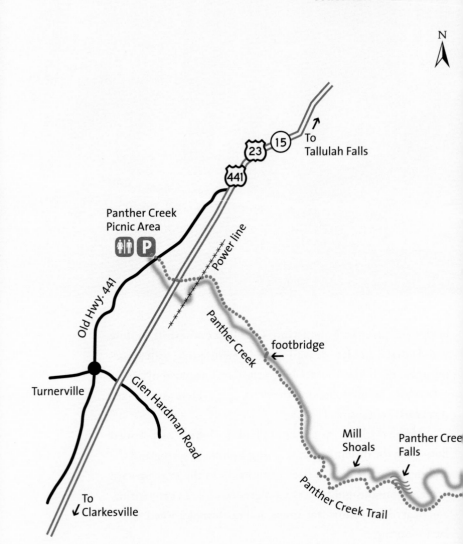

Green-and-gold (*Chrysogonum virginianum*)

With hairy oval leaves and bright gold 1- to 1.5-inch composite flower heads, green-and-gold forms a pleasing low ground cover in well-drained open woodlands. The rosettes of leaves send out runners that root at the leaf nodes, so the clumps spread easily. The flower heads usually have only five ray flowers, broadly oval and notched at the ends. The smaller disc flowers are a deeper gold, with dark stamens. Only the ray flowers form seeds, one each.

When they first appear in March, the flowers rest upon the leaves, but by June their stalks elongate and lift them 4 inches or more above. Green-and-gold often continues blooming sporadically throughout the summer.

As the trail follows the creek, the rushing water below crashes over rocks. From here to where the trail turns left to scramble up to a rock ledge (look for the double blue blazes), **gaywings** flank the trail in spring. These little pink airplane-shaped blooms appear here and there along the trail almost to the waterfall. The only other place we have seen them in Georgia is at nearby Tallulah Gorge State Park. As the trail continues along a bluff, **sweet white violets** appear on the ledges in spring. **Mountain laurel, Solomon's-plume, lady-rue,** and **common blue violet** also bloom along this stretch in spring.

After the scramble over the ledge, you face a relatively easy 0.25-mile walk to a bridge crossing Panther Creek. Look for yellow **spear-leaved violets** along here in spring. At the bottom of the

Trailing arbutus
(*Epigaea repens*)

Trailing arbutus is actually a prostrate evergreen shrub with alternate leathery oval leaves borne on woody stems covered with bristly hairs. It prefers rather dry rocky or sandy slopes with acid soils. It forms an association with a particular fungus that must be present in its soil, so it is difficult to transplant. Ants disperse the seeds.

According to legend, this was the first flower the Pilgrims found after arriving in the New World, and they called it mayflower after their ship. Its fragrant clusters of five-petaled pink or white flowers have been gathered for spring bouquets, and Native Americans used the leaves to treat a variety of complaints including kidney stones, indigestion, and rheumatism. Unfortunately, because it spreads slowly and is difficult to propagate, it began to disappear in the wild. In many states, picking it is now illegal.

Gaywings
(*Polygala paucifolia*)

Fringed polygala and bird-on-the-wing are other names for this charming pink or purple orchidlike flower. There are five sepals, three of them inconspicuous and the two lateral ones forming wings. The three petals are fused into a tube with yellow or pink fringe at the end. The whole flower resembles a miniature pink airplane complete with propeller.

Stems creeping beneath the leaf litter or underground send up short branches with three to six oval leaves near the top and smaller ▸▸

scalelike leaves below. One to four flowers grow from branch tips, producing small two-seeded fruits. In summer and fall, tiny closed self-pollinating flowers form additional fruits on the underground or covered stems.

Catesby's trillium (*Trillium catesbaei*)

A common trillium of mixed hardwood–pine forests of the mountains and Piedmont, Catesby's trillium has three petals that are white when the flower opens but turn pink to rose with age. Other common names for Catesby's trillium include rose trillium and rose wake-robin. The petals, the three narrow green sepals, and the anthers with twisted yellow pollen sacs all bend outward. The flower stalk droops, so that the flower is level with or below the whorl of three elliptical leaves. A tall stem holds leaves and flower 8 to 20 inches above the ground.

The species name honors Mark Catesby, an English naturalist who, in the early eighteenth century, journeyed through southeastern North America, observing, drawing, and collecting plants and animals, later publishing his *Natural History of Carolina, Georgia, Florida, and the Bahama Islands*.

slope is a campsite denuded of vegetation. Off to the left, however, the white- or pink-petaled flowers of **Catesby's trillium** nod on long stems. After crossing the bridge, the trail turns left and continues level for about a mile. The delicate white blossoms of **serviceberry** are among the first to be seen here in spring. A bit later,

Partridge berry (*Mitchella repens*)

Creeping stems with pairs of rounded evergreen leaves make partridge berry a natural ground cover in forested areas. It is not aggressive but slowly forms attractive low mats. Pairs of flowers form at the ends of branches and in leaf axils. The pink buds open into white flowers of four petals joined into a long tube at the base and flaring into four lobes at the tip. All flowers on each plant have either short hidden anthers and a protruding stigma, or the reverse, an arrangement that insures cross-pollination by the bumblebees that visit. Each pair of flowers forms a single bright red berry with two little circles at its end, the remnants of the sepals from each blossom.

The berries are nearly tasteless, but ground-feeding birds such as grouse, turkeys, and quail eat them.

Appalachian bellwort, **wood anemone**, **Indian cucumber-root**, **foamflower**, **mayapple**, **Jack-in-the-pulpit**, **strawberry bush**, **Solomon's-seal**, and **pink lady's-slipper** appear. Look up high in the trees to spot the orange-red trumpets of **cross-vine**. In summer **fire pink**, **partridge berry**, and **pipsissewa** bloom along this section of trail. Other summer flowers include **whorled loosestrife** and **hairy skullcap**.

The next stop on the trail is Mill Shoals, which you might mistake for the waterfall, but the grand waterfall is still a little less than a mile away. From the large rock overlooking the shoals, you can find **serviceberry** next to the rock and across Panther Creek. After a breather to admire the shoals, continue on the trail as it ascends several bluffs and descends again along turns in the creek. **Dimpled trout-lilies** will show up in early spring, while **gaywings, blue-star, wild geranium, Piedmont azalea,** and **blue phlox** emerge here a little later.

At Panther Creek Falls, the trail curves around beside the waterfall and drops steeply to a level spot worn bare by campers and picnickers. This slope has eroded considerably but does have a sturdy cable handrail. Be cautious, but don't miss the **dimpled trout-lilies** scattered down the slope in early spring. At the foot of the falls there is a nice pool with a sandy beach, a great place to have lunch and enjoy the scene. From here retrace your steps for 3.5 miles back to your car.

Fall brings a new ambiance to the trail. As one might expect with **red maples** in the area, leaf color is abundant. **Asters** and **goldenrods** form drifts of blue, white, and yellow. Near the beginning of the trail, **bunchflower** lifts airy panicles of white flowers above clumps of grasslike leaves. Prostrate stems of **partridge berry** sport bright red berries, which stand out against evergreen leaves. **Lobelias** bloom at this time too, and pinkish-white **turtleheads** arch on long branches close to the creek. Two members of the Indian-pipe family, **pine-sap** and **Indian-pipe,** raise their translucent upside-down pipes of orange or white along the trail in this season. Having no chlorophyll to produce food, they live on organic matter in the soil.

12
Bradley Peak Trail
Davidson–Arabia Mountain Nature Preserve

Flowering Season	March through October
Peak Flowering	Mid-April, September, and October
Walk Length	1.2 miles round-trip
Walk Rating	Easy gradual climb of 154 feet to peak
Restrooms	Primitive at south parking lot, better at Nature Center during hours of operation
Fee	None

Directions From I-20, take Lithonia exit 74 (Evans Mill Road) south. After one block, Evans Mill Road turns right at the traffic light. Continue straight through this intersection on to Woodrow Drive and drive about 1 mile to Klondike Road (T intersection). Turn right (south) on Klondike Road. The Nature Center is on the right at 3787 Klondike Road. About a mile farther south is the south parking lot and trailhead on the left (east) side of the road.

Environment This walk explores one of the outstanding granitic outcrops of the Georgia Piedmont. They were formed when magma intruded into preexisting country rock about 300 to 350 million years ago and cooled and solidified 10 miles or more beneath the surface. Over millions of years the land was uplifted, and the overlying rock eroded away to expose the granitic outcrops. There are two types: flatrock areas and monadnock domes (Wyatt and Allison 2000). Bradley Peak is one of the domes.

The outcrops have areas of bare rock interspersed with areas of very thin, sandy, or gravelly soil. They lose 95 percent of rainfall as runoff. Temperatures in midsummer can be extreme, registering 120 degrees Farenheit or more at the rock surface. Thus the outcrops are essentially desert environments.

Plants there must be adapted to the desert conditions. Some are succulent, storing water in fleshy stems and leaves. Some have hairy leaves and stems that may reflect sunlight and reduce water loss, or linear or finely dissected leaves that may reduce heat gain. Many are winter annuals, finishing their life cycles before summer's heat and drought.

Not all outcrops are composed entirely of granite. Some are made up of several related rock types. On Bradley Peak the basic underlying rock is biotite gneiss banded with lighter-colored granite formed when the gneiss was subjected to further high temperature and pressure in a later geologic event (Costello 2004). This rock surface has weathered into depressions with soil of varying depths, wherein spectacular "dish gardens" bloom. Some depressions hold water in the rainy season and are called vernal pools.

The Walk   From the information kiosk at the trail entrance, the path proceeds through woods for about 10 yards before reach-

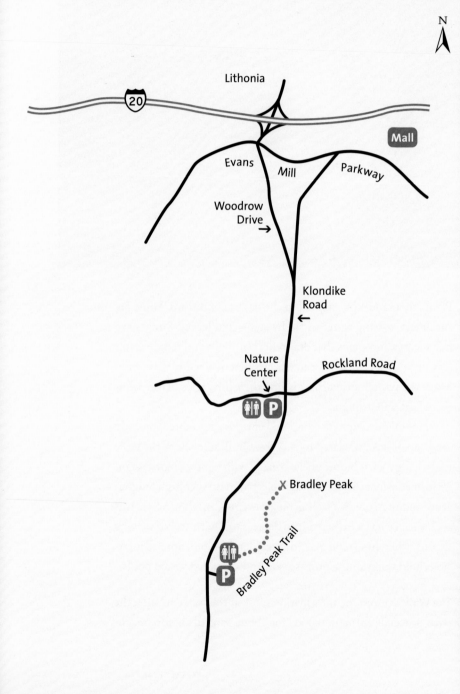

BRADLEY PEAK TRAIL

N

Lithonia

20

Mall

Evans   Mill   Parkway

Woodrow
Drive

Klondike
Road

Nature
Center   Rockland Road

Bradley Peak

Bradley Peak Trail

Snorkelwort (*Amphianthus pusillus*)

One of the rarest of the outcrop plants, snorkelwort is adapted to a very specific and uncommon habitat. It grows only on the Piedmont Plateau in Alabama, Georgia, and South Carolina, in vernal pools on granitic outcrops. Moreover, the pool must have a level bottom with about 2 inches of accumulated soil, be less than 1 foot deep, and be entirely surrounded by bare rock. No wonder it is so rare.

As an annual, snorkelwort must complete its entire life cycle in the short period before summer heat dries out the pools. It forms a rosette of tiny leaves at the bottom of the pool, then sends up several threadlike stems, each topped with a pair of tiny oval leaves cradling a single diminutive white to pale violet flower. The appearance of the floating leaves and flowers has led to the common name, snorklewort.

The floating flowers may be cross-pollinated, but the plant doesn't depend solely upon these to produce seed. Among the cluster of leaves at the bottom of the pool are other tiny flowers that are self-pollinated. Recent genetic studies suggest that most of the seed is produced by self-pollination, leading to little genetic diversity. Snorkelwort is very vulnerable to any changes in its environment, including foot and bicycle traffic when the pools are dry, and many sites have been lost to quarrying.

Elf-orpine
(*Diamorpha smallii*)

In early spring, depressions on the granitic outcrops turn an eye-catching red when colonies of elf-orpine flourish in preparation for flowering. The red succulent leaves and stems may form a dense 2-inch-thick mat on the shallow soil. Soon white flowers with four (occasionally five) petals appear at the tips of the short branches.

Elf-orpine has developed a successful strategy for survival in the severe conditions of granitic outcrops of the Piedmont of the Southeast. Its seeds sprout in late fall when rain is plentiful and form tiny rosettes of succulent reddish green leaves that remain through the winter. In spring it quickly shoots up to about 3 inches, produces flowers and seeds, and then dies by late spring. But the seeds do not germinate until fall brings cooler, moister conditions more favorable for seedlings.

ing the exposed rock. At the edge of the woods are **Ohio spiderworts**, bright blue-petaled flowers. A related spiderwort on some other outcrops is hairy, rather than smooth like this one. Also at the beginning of the trail is the **hairy groundsel** with yellow composite flowers. The rock path is designated by rock cairns from here all the way to the top of Bradley Peak. **It is important to stay close to the path to avoid damaging small plants that are tiny and inconspicuous or are dormant, particularly in the depressions.** This area displays evidence of earlier quarrying, one of the reasons why rock outcrops are becoming so rare.

The path meanders among delightful dish gardens. One near the beginning provides an especially good example of the way plants arrange themselves according to differing depths of soil.

Confederate daisy
(*Helianthus porteri*, synonym *Viguiera porteri*)

Also known as Stone Mountain daisy, Confederate daisy forms great drifts of gold on granitic outcrops of Georgia and Alabama from September into October. Up to 3 feet tall, with narrow leaves and many-branched stems, it bears numerous flower heads about 1.5 inches across. The ray flowers are a golden yellow, while the conical disc bears tiny yellow flowers with brown anthers.

This large plant's abundant flowering is amazing considering it is an annual that does not germinate until spring and produces most of its growth during the hot dry days of summer. It does seed prolifically during normal years, and if the rains fail and few seeds are produced one year, some seeds from previous years may remain in the soil and be able to grow the next year.

Hairy groundsel
(*Packera tomentosa*, synonym *Senecio tomentosus*)

Many daisylike flowers with bright yellow discs and rays top the many-branched stem that rises from a group of stiffly upright oval leaves. Hairy groundsel's lower stem and the backs of its basal leaves are covered with soft, cottony white hairs, giving it another common name, cottony groundsel. Found in moderately deep soils of depression pits on Piedmont granitic outcrops, hairy groundsel also grows in moist sandy soils of the Coastal Plain from New Jersey to Texas.

Sunnybell
(*Schoenolirion croceum*)

The charming common name leads us to expect a pretty plant, and so it is. The single stem, up to 1.5 feet tall, has many flowers, the lower ones opening first. Each flower has six quarter-inch-long yellow tepals (sepals and petals) and attaches to the stem by a stalk. Leaves are narrow and grasslike, clustered at the base of the stem. The stem itself is leafless, but narrow leaflike bracts arise where each flower stalk attaches to the stem.

Sunnybell grows from a perennial bulb in drainage areas and wet pockets of the granitic outcrops. It is also found in wet sandy spots on the Coastal Plain from Florida to Texas.

The outer edge with the thinnest soil is filled with an annual, **elf-orpine**. This dramatic plant has red succulent stems and leaves that set off flowers of four white petals. A bit further in, where there is a little more soil, grows **sandwort**, another white-flowered annual, with blossoms massed into a nearly solid band of white. Nearer the middle of the "garden," with still more soil, are grasses such as **chalky broomsedge**. Here also are **sunnybells** with racemes of yellow flowers. In the center of the depression, the soil is deep enough that a small **loblolly pine** tree has grown.

Soon the path makes a sharp left turn around a vernal pool where the rare **snorkelwort** occurs. Its extremely small flower, held up by two small leaves floating on the water, is hard to see. Do not miss the **bear-grass** growing in some of the dish gardens. The yellow-flowered vine growing on trees is **yellow jasmine**. You will find it again at the summit.

As the trail ascends more steeply, the dish gardens are scattered all along the slope. These gardens feature a succession of blooms at different times of year. In early spring **elf-orpine, sandwort, sunnybells,** and **Ohio spiderwort** flower. Later **large-flowered coreopsis, false-pimpernel,** and **sundrops** appear. Midsummer brings **meadow-beauty, large-flowered coreopsis, sundrops, slender dayflower, ironweed, Curtiss's milkwort,** and **yellow-eyed-grass. Winged sumac** will also be in bloom. Fall brings the massed golden blooms of **Confederate daisy** in a spectacular display.

At the summit there are a few dish gardens containing **yellow jasmine, Ohio spiderwort,** and **toadflax,** as well as several large vernal pools. In spring look especially carefully there for **snorkelwort.** By summer the pools may be completely dried up, but the **snorkelworts** will have completed their life cycle and produced seed for the following year.

Return the way you came. On the way down look for **sparkleberry** bushes, which bloom in the spring and produce unpalatable blueberries in late summer. Another spring-blooming shrub here is **serviceberry.**

Although the peak bloom for this trail is mid-April, with a second peak in fall for **Confederate daisy,** this is a wonderful walk any time of year, thanks to the expansive views from Bradley Peak.

13
Blue Trail
Rock and Shoals Outcrop Natural Area

Flowering Season	March through October
Peak Flowering	Mid-April
Walk Length	0.4 mile
Walk Rating	Easy
Restrooms	None
Fee	None

Directions

From Athens take Milledge Avenue south past the Ga. 10 Loop and the State Botanical Garden of Georgia. (You may want to stop for restrooms at the garden, since there are none at the site). Continue south on Milledge until you come to a fork. Take the left fork and immediately turn left onto Whitehall Road. Cross the Oconee River and go up the hill to the first traffic light. Turn right on Barnett Shoals Road and pass Barnett Shoals School. On the right, about a mile past the school, is Rock and Shoals subdivision, with a pile of boulders at the entrance. Turn right and go to the end of the paved road. Park on the road. The trailhead, with a mailbox that contains maps, is on the right along the muddy continuation of the road before it reaches a chain-link fence. Rough stairs descend to a path marked with blue flagging, which leads to a small outcrop.

Environment

Rock and Shoals is another Piedmont granitic outcrop, but this one is a flatrock, not a dome. The walk passes through a successional oak–pine forest with understory dominated by **eastern hophornbeam**. Aerial photos show cotton fields here in the 1930s. The terraces are still visible on the hillside above the trail. The walk follows a stream, crosses at a lovely cascade, and proceeds through more open woods with **eastern red-cedar** and grasses to a small outlying outcrop. In this bare rock

community, very little soil has accumulated. In somewhat deeper soils, still too thin for woody plants, a patchy grass–herb community occurs.

The Walk   The steep stairs to the beginning of the path have no handrail, so please be careful. There are few wildflowers as the path passes through the oak–pine woodland. Nonetheless, in

False-pimpernel (*Lindernia monticola*)

One must look closely to see the details of false-pimpernel's tiny blooms. They are divided into two lips, the smaller upper one with two lobes, the lower one with three. They are lavender to white and marked with intricate violet spots, streaks, and edgings. Flower stems, usually with a single bloom, arise from a rosette of small oval leaves.

False-pimpernel prefers depression pits that hold water for a long time after rains or seepy areas with a steady supply of water. It flowers from April to June, but as long as there is enough water, it continues to bloom sporadically into fall. It occurs mostly on granitic outcrops but also, rarely, in wet sandy habitats in the Coastal Plain.

spring **Catesby's trillium** blooms and in summer **cranefly orchid** may be found. **Christmas fern** grows on the banks of the stream, while on the flat areas above it, **rattlesnake fern** grows in spring, and **southern grapefern** grows in late fall. At one spot by the edge of the stream, a colony of **mayapple** blooms in spring. The path crosses the stream just above the cascade. Below the cascade, note a nice stand of native **cane**. Follow the path up the hill, where it turns left into more open woods of **eastern redcedar** with grasses, rock rubble, and small boulders covering the ground. The grasses include **needle grass**, which flowers in spring and produces sharp-needled seeds soon after, and **woodoats**, which produces long, arching stalks bearing small seeds in late summer. Many wildflowers show up here. Amid the grasses in spring are **spotted phacelia, blephilia, false-garlic, southeastern beard-tongue, longleaf bluets, common wild petunia,** and **hairystem spiderwort.**

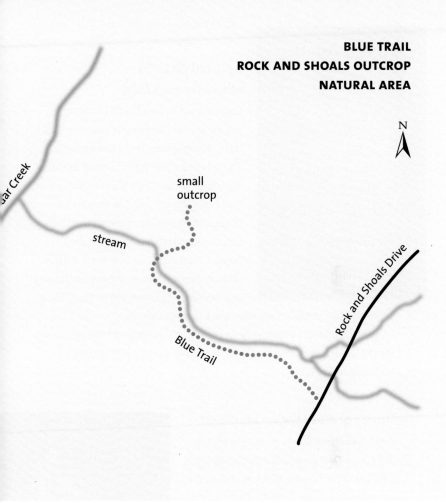

N

small outcrop

stream

Blue Trail

Rock and Shoals Drive

ar Creek

Summer walks reveal **elephant's-foot** and **blackberry-lily**, a non-native that has become naturalized in outcrop areas. In the fall, **false-garlic** returns, and **tickweed** will also be blooming.

As you emerge into the open rock area, notice the lichens—**peppered rock-shield**—and mosses—**grimmia**—growing where there is almost no soil. The blue-gray tones of **peppered rock-shield** are most vivid in winter and early spring or anytime conditions have been moist for a few days. **Grimmia** is bright green touched with silver when wet, but turns silvery black when dry.

Spotted phacelia (*Phacelia maculata*)

Each of the five pale bluish to lavender petals has two dark purple spots near its base, giving spotted phacelia its name. The leaves are divided into many leaflets. The rather weak stems may stand erect or trail along the ground. The flowers are borne in a cluster along the stem, which unfurls like a fern fiddlehead as the flowers bloom. By the time those on the tip have opened, the stem has straightened out. Because the coiled stems resemble a scorpion's tail, phacelias are also called scorpion weeds.

Spotted phacelia grows only on the granitic outcrops of the Southeast. Most phacelias are western plants, with only about seven species occurring in the East.

Puck's orpine (*Sedum pusillum*)

A rare plant found only on the Piedmont Plateau of Georgia and North and South Carolina, Puck's orpine looks much like the common elf-orpine. Both are short plants with succulent leaves and stems, topped with clusters of white, four-petaled flowers. But while the stems and leaves of elf-orpine are usually red, those of Puck's orpine are usually blue-green though they can be reddish if the plant grows in full sun. The two plants were considered the same species until 1875, when botanist Asa Gray saw both species growing ▶▶

near each other at Stone Mountain and documented their differences. In fact, the two have very different numbers of chromosomes and do not hybridize.

Puck's orpine prefers shadier sites than elf-orpine. It is usually found in shallow soil on flatrock outcrops nestled among mosses in the shade of old eastern redcedars.

Appalachian fameflower (*Phemeranthus teretifolius*, synonym *Talinum teretifolium*)

It can be hard to catch Appalachian fameflower in bloom. Each flower opens for only a few hours in late afternoon on a single day. On overcast days it does not open. The five-petaled rose pink flowers bloom in open clusters upon a stem up to a foot long. The pistil is the same length as the fifteen to twenty stamens, and if the flower is not cross-pollinated, it will self-pollinate when it closes. (In a rarer species, *Phemeranthus mengesii*, the pistil is much longer than the fifty to ninety stamens, and the larger flower does not self-pollinate.) Narrow succulent leaves 1.5 to 2 inches long crowd the bottom of the stem. The species name, *teretifolius*, comes from the shape of the leaves, *terete* meaning round in cross section, and *folius* meaning leaf.

Appalachian fameflower can be found on outcrops of many kinds of acidic rock throughout the Southeast. Although it grows in very thin dry soil, it is a perennial with a branched rootstock that survives from year to year.

Children (of all ages) enjoy watching the dry moss turn green before their eyes when they pour a bit of water from a canteen onto it.

Around the edges of the rock, in thin soil, **small bluets** and **sandworts** bloom in early spring. In deeper soil, **prickly-pear** blooms with large, bright yellow flowers. The **hairystem spiderwort** seems to like the grassy, open woods area, as well as sunny sites near boulders or fire ant hills. During late spring and summer, **Appalachian fameflower** blooms. A late summer plant, **rushfoil**, has a minute flower, but its beautiful copper-colored foliage is conspicuous in fall.

Adjacent to the open rock area, with somewhat deeper soils, is a grassy-herb area. The dominant grass is **little bluestem**, and among the grasses in spring will be **southern ragwort** and **false-pimpernel**. In late spring and summer, **false-dandelion** and **large-flowered coreopsis** can be found here. The little fern snuggled among the rocks is **hairy lipfern**. During dry spells it turns brown but quickly greens up again when moister conditions return.

Where the trail first emerges into the open rock area, look for a small outcrop to the left (west) just beyond a little seep. Here the flatrock is shaded by **eastern redcedars** and is covered with **hedwigia moss**. **Early saxifrage**, one of the first plants to bloom, and the infrequent **Puck's orpine** can be found in this location in early spring.

Before returning to the trailhead, take one last look at the rock and imagine it in different seasons and times of day. Early morning sparkles with dew on grasses and **eastern redcedars**. After rains, the mosses are a bright green. In winter the lichens and mosses are their most colorful, while in summer drought the **grimmia** is gray, and the lichens are dry and brittle. In spring, flowers are blooming in whites, blues, and yellows. In fall the copper of the **rushfoil** colors the landscape. Carry these images with you as you head back down the blue-flagged trail.

Hairystem spiderwort (*Tradescantia hirsuticaulis*)

This spiderwort has three equal petals of purple to rose pink or occasionally white, contrasting with five or six bright yellow anthers on densely hairy filaments. Sepals, leaves, and stems are also hairy. The leaves, arising alternately from the stem, are narrow with parallel veins and are folded in the middle.

The name spiderwort may refer to the way the narrow basal leaves bend in the middle so that the tips touch the ground, resembling a spider's legs. It may also refer to the way the sap from a broken stem forms strands like a spider's web. Spiderworts are also sometimes called dayflowers because each flower lasts but one day. The genus honors John Tradescant, gardener to Charles I. The hairystem spiderwort grows in dry woods and rocky areas in the Piedmont from North Carolina to Alabama.

14
West Palisades Trail
Chattahoochee River National Recreation Area

Flowering Season	March through October
Peak Flowering	Early March through April
Walk Length	1 mile
Walk Rating	Easy, except for steep ascent with about 100-foot elevation change from river back to parking area
Restrooms	On the north end of the loop near the old road
Fee	Parking fee

Directions *Going west on I-285*: Take exit 22 (Northside Drive). From ramp go straight through first traffic light (New Northside Drive) to second light (Northside Drive). Turn left, cross over highway, and continue to next street, Powers Ferry Road. *Going east on I-285*: Take exit 22 and turn right on Northside Drive from ramp.

Turn right on Powers Ferry Road. At next light, continue straight onto Akers Mill Drive. In just over 0.5 mile, a waterwheel will be visible on the left. Turn left at the waterwheel onto Akers Drive. Near the top of the hill, a sign on the left indicates the parking area for the Chattahoochee National Recreation Area.

Environment The walk loops through an oak–pine Piedmont forest that is dry on the cliffs and moist in ravines and alluvial bottomland located along the Chattahoochee River. It is amazing that such a great woodland trail exists in the midst of the city of Atlanta, close to the intersection of I-75 and I-285. The many nearby apartment dwellers have a gem of a neighborhood walk. The rocky cliffs are beautiful any time of year. Although longer walks are possible within this section of the Chattahoochee National Recreation Area, this half-mile loop is the richest in wildflowers.

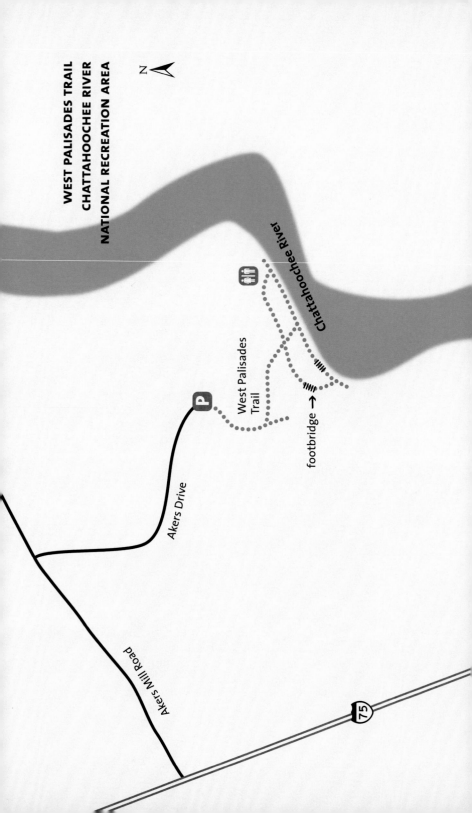

WEST PALISADES TRAIL
CHATTAHOOCHEE RIVER
NATIONAL RECREATION AREA

N

Chattahoochee River

West Palisades Trail

footbridge →

P

Akers Drive

Akers Mill Road

75

Blue-star
(*Amsonia tabernaemontana*)

Five pale blue petals with pointed tips give blue-stars their name. The flowers appear in clusters at the top of 2- to 4-foot stems with oval or lance-shaped leaves. Usually they form handsome groups of several many-stemmed plants in moist open woodlands or along stream banks.

Blue-stars belong to the dogbane family, so called because these plants were thought to be poisonous to dogs. One member, oleander, is extremely poisonous.

The Latin name honors two men: Charles Amson, a physician of Glouster County, Virginia, and Jakob Theodor von Bergzabern—who preferred Tabernaemontanus, the latinized form of Bergzabern—physician to the Count of the Palatine at Heidelberg and author of a celebrated herbal.

The Walk From the parking area, the path follows an old road down the ravine to the bottomland area. Several dirt paths branch off with no signage. Skip the first worn path to the left and then another to the right. Stay on the road as it turns to the left and goes steeply downhill on rough pavement for about 0.25 mile. In early spring not much is in flower along here. At the bottom of the hill, take the first trail to the right, beginning a loop through the bottomland. Early in spring, **sweet Betsy** will be starting to flower on both sides of the trail. The showy white flowers of **bloodroot** will be more conspicuous and more plentiful than **sweet Betsy**. A little further on, **dimpled trout-lilies** begin to appear, but after you cross a small stream, look up the slope to your right. At their peak flowering there are **dimpled**

Dimpled trout-lily
(*Erythronium umbilicatum*)

A carpet of pointed leaves mottled in shades of green and maroon spreads along stream banks and moist wooded slopes in early spring. Soon each pair of leaves sends up a single stalk with a miniature yellow lily. The insides of the three petals and three sepals are spotted with maroon, while the exteriors of the sepals are pale maroon, and the petals have a maroon stripe along the outer midrib. Both sepals and petals curve strongly backward. The flowers open in the sunlight and close at night. The plants arise from a small corm buried deep in the ground. The corms send out thready underground branches, forming new corms at their tips. These produce only a single leaf and no flower for several years.

Naturalist John Burroughs said the trout-lily was so named because it is found along trout streams and its leaf resembles a trout's mottled back. Other common names are fawn lily, adder's tongue, and dog-tooth violet.

trout-lilies by the thousands spread as far as the eye can see. In among the **dimpled trout-lilies** are **toothworts** and **heart-leaf**. Also blooming along this section of the trail are **round-lobed liverleaf** and **green-and-gold**. Although the diversity of species is limited, the display is spectacular and not to be missed.

As the trail turns toward the river, look for a path going off to the left. This crosses the small stream on a footbridge and continues along the river, eventually turning away from it to return to the old road and complete the loop. Some times of year, especially in early spring, the riverside section of the loop cannot be walked

Featherbells
(*Stenanthium gramineum*)

Tall, many-branched stems are crowded with small, nodding white or greenish flowers. The pointed, narrow sepals and petals give the inflorescence a feathery look (*Stenanthium* means "narrow flower"). Thin grasslike leaves, folded along the midrib, cluster at the base and continue up the stem.

Featherbells flower from June to September in open, rocky woods with acid soils. They are occasional plants, occurring in scattered locations, often in small colonies. Finding a flowering group is always a pleasure.

Giant chickweed
(*Stellaria pubera*)

Look closely at the petals of giant chickweed. At first glance there appear to be ten, but in reality there are only five, split down the middle nearly to the base. The plants form neat clumps with several pairs of oval leaves on erect stems 6 to 12 inches tall, with flowers in clusters at the tops.

Called chickweeds because chickens like to peck at their seeds, some species are weedy. Common chickweed is an introduced lawn weed that grows nearly year-round throughout the Southeast. Giant chickweed, however, is a native species found in rich woods. It spreads slowly, forming mounds of dark green leaves that contrast with multitudes of little white starry flowers. It is sometimes called starry chickweed.

because it is flooded. In that case walk back the way you came and take the road until it reaches the north end of the loop.

Some **dimpled trout-lilies** can still be seen on the first section of the loop later in spring, but new species are added to the display: **serviceberry**, a shrub with clusters of dainty white flowers; **yellow jasmine**, a vine; **rue-anemone**; **cleft-leaved violet**; **giant chickweed**; and another shrub, **red buckeye**. Close to the river patches of **yellow-root** dangle panicles of tiny maroon flowers.

Later in spring the **dimpled trout-lilies** are gone. But now flowers appear along the first part of the trail as the old road descends the slope. Blossoms of **flowering dogwood** seem to float in the forest understory. **Rattlesnake-weed, deerberry**, and **yellow wood-sorrel** dot the edges of the road. On the floodplain, new blooms join the many plants seen earlier: **Catesby's trillium, violet wood-sorrel, wild geranium, Solomon's-plume, Solomon's-seal, foamflower, Jack-in-the-pulpit, mountain laurel, sweet-shrub**, and **common silverbell**, a small tree. Along the river look for **blue-star, daisy fleabane, Piedmont azalea**, and **dog-hobble**.

By mid-May the early spring flowers are gone. A number of plants may be flowering, but they are not as profuse or diverse as earlier in the season. Flowers along the trail now include **heartleaf skullcap, goat's-rue, fire pink, Indian-physic, Ohio spiderwort, racemed milkwort, hairy phlox, Indian-pink, fringed loosestrife**, and **pipsissewa**.

During summer the open sunny areas along the path bloom with **sunflowers** and **goldenrods**. In shadier areas look for **cranefly orchid, pencil-flower, yellow leafcup, yellow passion-flower**, and **featherbells**. **Elephant's-foot**, a typical plant of Piedmont forests, is in flower.

In fall **elephant's-foot** is joined by its close relative, **leafy-stemmed elephant's-foot**. The berries of the **strawberry bush**,

Sweet Betsy
(*Trillium cuneatum*)

The most common trillium of the Piedmont, sweet Betsy is one of the purple toadshades, with maroon (occasionally green or yellow) flowers and three mottled leaves. While some toadshades stink like carrion to attract flies and beetles as pollinators, sweet Betsy has a pleasant fragrance and is bee pollinated.

A trillium seedling takes about seven years to reach flowering size. Young plants have a single, small ground-hugging leaf, while somewhat older plants have three small leaves but do not flower. Displays of large numbers of blooming trilliums are becoming rarer as increasing deer populations graze them, people dig them up, and development destroys their habitats.

or hearts-a-burstin', can be found on the road down from the parking lot. The river section of the trail has the most flowers now: **sunflowers, goldenrods, northern horse-balm, wood aster, wingstem, tickweed, downy lobelia, golden-aster,** and **iron-weed.**

15
White Trail
Sweetwater Creek State Conservation Park

Flowering Season	March through October
Peak Flowering	Throughout flowering season
Walk Length	6 miles out and back on the White Trail
	4 miles combining Red and White Trails in loop
Walk Rating	*White Trail:* Easy except for gradual ascent of 270 feet returning from bottom of falls to parking area.
	Red Trail: Moderate, but along Sweetwater Creek, roots, boulders, and stairs require constant attention.
Restrooms	At trailhead parking lot
Fee	Parking fee
Directions	Drive west from Atlanta on I-20 to exit 44. Go left from the off-ramp on Ga. 6 for 0.4 mile to South Blairs Bridge Road. Turn right onto South Blairs Bridge Road; go 2.1 miles to Mt. Vernon Road. Take a left on Mt. Vernon Road, enter the park, and take a left on Factory Shoals Road; continue to trailhead parking and Visitor Center at the end of the road.
Environment	From the trailhead, the White Trail passes through the picnic area before following an old dirt road through a typical Piedmont dry upland oak–pine woods. Near an old homestead, the path turns right and crosses a grassy area. A profusion of daffodils crowds the remaining foundations of the house in spring. At the end of the grassy area, the trail descends on a moderate slope through more oak–pine woods to Jack's Hill Lake, where ducks paddle, an occasional great blue heron hunts for food, and turtles sunbathe on floating logs. Then the path enters a cove and follows the stream draining the lake. Vegetation more common to the mountains occurs here because of the shade and greater moisture levels. Rather than large numbers of a few species creating swaths of color, though, blooms

of many different plants are scattered about in each season. After reaching Sweetwater Creek the trail goes upstream to a waterfall marked by the overlook on the map.

The Walk   From the trailhead near the Visitor Center, take the White Trail through the picnic area for about 0.5 mile to the old roadway. In early spring, **bluets** and **Piedmont azaleas** bloom along the side of the road and also farther along the walk. The trail turns right through a grassy area and then re-enters the forest with another sharp right turn at a bench on the left. This begins a descent to the lake. **Trailing arbutus** starts flowering beside the trail in early spring. Also along this section of the trail look for **green-and-gold**, **dwarf cinquefoil**, **small bluet**, **pussytoes**, **robins-plantain**, and **bloodroot**.

At the end of the lake, the path jogs right until it reaches stairs that take you down to the left into a lovely cove below the lake. Many more **bloodroot** are found here, and other early spring wildflowers abound: **heart-leaf**, **rue-anemone**, **wood**

WHITE TRAIL
SWEETWATER CREEK
STATE CONSERVATION PARK

To 20
N
George H. Sparks
Reservoir
Factory Shoals Road
Mt. Vernon Road
P
Picnic
Area
To 92
Sweetwater Creek
Red Trail
Factory Ruins
White Trail
Overlook
Jack's Hill Lake
White Trail

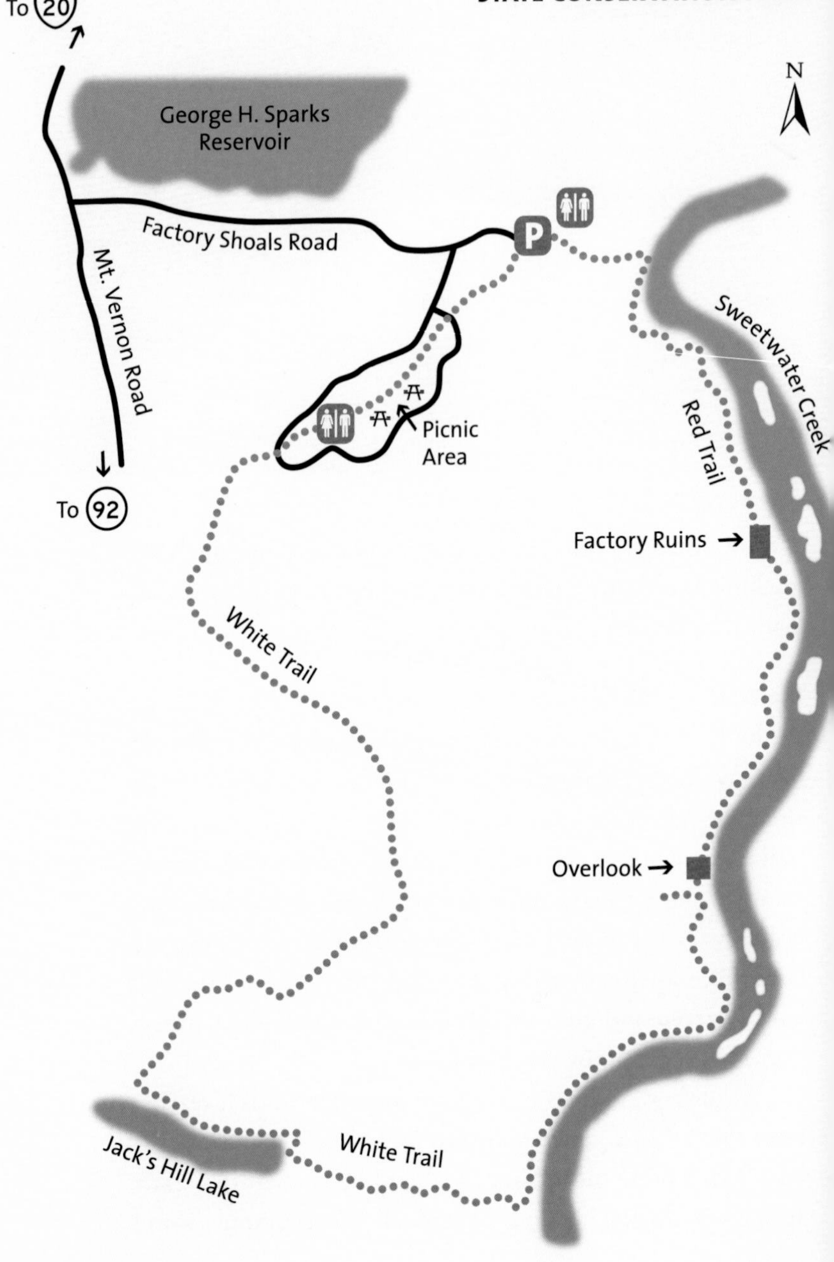

Rue-anemone
(*Anemonella thalictroides*,
synonym *Thalictrum thalictroides*)

The name anemone comes from the Greek word for wind, and *Anemonella* is a diminutive form, meaning "little anemone," or "little windflower." The dainty flowers of rue-anemone dance in the breeze on slender stems. The compound leaves have three leaflets with three rounded lobes at their tips. What appear to be five to ten white petals are actually sepals. One to five flowers cluster in loose umbels at the top of the stem.

One of the first of the spring wildflowers, it also has one of the longest flowering periods. It ignores March freezes and continues to produce new blooms well into May. Rue-anemone is common in rich woods and on stream banks in the mountains and Piedmont. A perennial, it grows from starchy tuberous roots that in some places have been boiled and eaten, but some plants may be toxic.

anemone, **giant chickweed**, **round-lobed liverleaf**, **spear-leaved violets**, and by the stream, **yellow-root**. **Painted buckeye** blooms in the understory; some botanists think those in this cove might be hybrids with red buckeye. Ferns, including large **cinnamon ferns**, spread throughout the cove. At Sweetwater Creek (really a river), you could turn left and go up the path to the waterfall, then follow the Red Trail to return to the trailhead (1.5 miles). The Red Trail passes the ruins of the New Manchester Manufacturing Company, a textile mill burned during the Civil War. In March **dimpled trout-lilies** flower on the slopes beside the ruins. On the other hand, you could turn around and return by the same White Trail to the trailhead (2.5 miles).

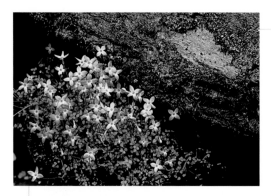

Bluets
(*Houstonia caerulea*)

Quaker ladies and
innocence are other names
bluets' neat simplicity
have earned them. The
pale blue flowers have
four petals joined into a
short tube at the base, then flaring at right angles to the tube to make a
flat face with a yellow center, or eye. Flowers are borne singly on stems
arising from a clump of small oval leaves. To prevent self-pollination,
flowers of an individual plant have either long pollen-bearing stamens
and very short seed-producing pistils or long pistils and very short
stamens. Bluets often form dense mats in damp but well-drained spots
in clearings or open woodlands.

The genus name refers to William Houston, a Scottish botanist and
physician who collected plants of Mexico and the West Indies while
serving as a ship's surgeon.

Round-lobed liverleaf
(*Anemone americana*, synonym *Hepatica nobilis* var. *obtusa*)

The evergreen basal leaves
have three rounded lobes,
green on top, purple
underneath. The flowers,
which appear before the new spring leaves, have up to twelve petal-like
sepals of purple, blue, or white, which open in the morning and close at
night. They are pollinated by flying insects such as bees and flies, but the
seeds are dispersed by ants.

Because the shape of the leaves somewhat resembles the human liver, they were believed, erroneously, to be helpful in treating liver problems. In the 1880s liverleaf was an ingredient in popular patent medicines. The demand was so great that American collectors could not supply enough, and more than 400,000 pounds were imported from Germany in a single year.

Hairy skullcap
(*Scutellaria elliptica*)

The bright blue to violet flowers of hairy skullcap are a delight to find in the deciduous woodland, especially since they appear from late May to July, after many woodland flowers have finished blooming. The tubular flowers have two lips, the upper one three-lobed and forming a helmet, the lower wide and rounded. They are borne on one to five racemes above an erect hairy stem that is square in cross section. Two to seven pairs of elliptic, scallop-edged leaves are widely spaced along the stem. The name skullcap refers to the upper, caplike part of the seed capsule. When the four seeds are ripe, the cover splits off, allowing the seeds to spill from the lower part.

Although it belongs to the mint family, hairy skullcap is not aromatic, and the leaves have a bitter flavor. The leaves of skullcaps have been used as mild nerve tonics. In the nineteenth century, one species, *Scutellaria laterifolia*, was believed to be a cure for hydrophobia, or rabies, acquiring the common name mad-dog skullcap.

Soapwort gentian
(*Gentiana saponaria*)

The upright flowers of soapwort gentian are formed from four to ten petals fused into a tube for about half their length. Above the tube the petals separate into lobes connected by tissue-thin material that forms a pleat. The petals spread only slightly at the tip, so that the flower never appears fully open. Stems have seven to fifteen pairs of oval leaves, with flowers in a terminal cluster and sometimes in the upper leaf axils.

Like many gentians, soapwort gentian is a late bloomer, adding its blue-purple color to the autumn shades of fallen foliage in wet areas. Both the common and scientific names refer to soapwort *(Saponaria officinalis)*, which has a lather-producing juice that ancient Greeks used as soap. The only similarity between the two plants is the shape of the leaves: soapwort gentian is not soapy.

In late spring, more flowers are found along the road and the descent to the lake than in the cove: **summer bluets, pipsissewa, Venus's looking-glass, daisy fleabane, lesser daisy fleabane, racemed milkwort, southern ragwort, yellow star-grass, hairy skullcap, Ohio spiderwort**, and **white milkweed**. In the cove, however, are **black snakeroot, flowering spurge, common American alumroot, Virginia willow**, and **St. Andrew's cross**.

In summer the same is true—more flowers grow along the road and down the slope than in the cove: **elephant's-foot, Asiatic dayflower, cranefly orchid, black-eyed-Susan, bitterweed, lance-leaved loosestrife, may-pop, yellow leafcup**, and **partridge-**

pea. Down in the cove **starry campion, pale Indian-plantain, yellow star-grass**, and **summer bluets** are blooming.

Many of these same flowers still appear in fall, but there are some new ones too: **hoary tick-trefoil, beggar-ticks, downy lobelia, northern horse-balm, rabbit-tobacco, grass-leaved golden-aster, golden-aster, paleleaf sunflower, woodland sunflower, fireweed, lady's-thumb, wood aster, southern harebell,** and **blazing-star.** The cove will be brightened with **white snakeroot** and the berries of **strawberry bush**, also called hearts-a-burstin' because the red fruit splits open to expose the orange seeds. In late fall we have found **soapwort gentian** flowering where the stream from Jack's Hill Lake meets Sweetwater Creek and all along Sweetwater Creek to the waterfall.

Any time is a good time for this trail. Even when no flowers are in bloom, the waterfall on Sweetwater Creek and the factory ruins are interesting destinations.

16
Hall's Bridge Tract #1
Ohoopee Dunes Natural Area

Flowering Season	March through October
Peak Flowering	May and September
Walk Length	2.25 miles
Walk Rating	Easy
Restrooms	None
Fee	None

Directions From Norristown drive north on U.S. 221/Ga. 171 for 1.1 miles to Hall's Bridge Road (C.R. 160). Take the second right turn north of Norristown (the road sign was missing at the time of this writing). Go right (east) on Hall's Bridge Road (unpaved) for 1.6 miles. The entrance to the Ohoopee Dunes Natural Area is on the left, just past the bridge over the Little Ohoopee River. Park on Hall's Bridge Road near the entrance and walk in. Some people drive the first leg, but the sand is deep in places, and it is easy to get stuck. Also, walking allows you to better observe the wildflowers. Be aware of hunting season dates, since hunting is allowed at this site.

Environment The unique parabolic shapes of the Ohoopee Dunes were first revealed on Landsat satellite images made in 1974. These curious dunes, made of coarse, windblown, riverine alluvial sand, are believed to have been formed during the late Pleistocene Age 20,000 years ago. They are located on the east side of the Ohoopee River, and similar dunes occur east of the Canoochee River (Wharton 1978). This tract of the Ohoopee Dunes Natural Area is covered by a dwarf oak–evergreen shrub forest. The many dwarf trees, unusual shrubs, and white sands strewn with mounded foamlike tufts of **reindeer lichen** give this area a unique character. On the first part of the walk, dwarfed **live**

oak trees will be on the left, whereas most of the area is covered by dwarfed **turkey oaks**. Here and there are **longleaf pines**. The most unusual plants are shrubs including **sandhill rosemary, red basil, Ohoopee Dunes wild basil**, and **bush goldenrod**.

The Walk   This walk forms a triangle. The first leg follows an unpaved road for about 0.7 mile. The second leg, about 0.9 mile, angles back to Hall's Bridge Road. The third leg, about 0.7 mile, follows Hall's Bridge Road back to the trailhead.

In early spring, **Chickasaw plum, toadflax**, and the **yellow jasmine** vine are in flower along the first leg. Later in spring this stretch yields **threadleaf sandhills blue-star, Carolina sun-rose, tread-softly, dyschoriste, Carolina sandwort, prickly-pear**, and **wiry bladderwort**.

In late summer and fall the road is even more colorful. **Red basil** in both its scarlet and yellow forms will be flowering, along with **threadleaf false-foxglove, seymeria, grassleaf blazing**

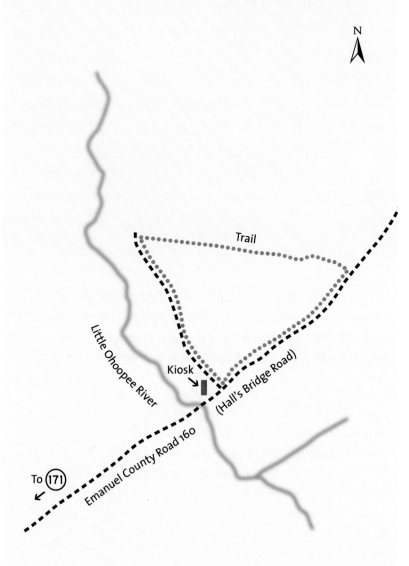

Threadleaf sandhills blue-star (*Amsonia ciliata* var. *tenuifolia*)

This species of blue-star is abundant in sandy soil of the inner Coastal Plain, in open areas or thin woods. Its clusters of pale blue, star-shaped flowers sit atop hairy stems with very narrow, 1- to 3-inch-long leaves. Each flower has five petals, united into a tube at the base. The tube is hairy on the inside but smooth on the outside.

Blue-stars belong to the dogbane family, whose members all have milky sap. The genus name honors Charles Amson, an eighteenth-century Virginia physician.

Lupine (*Lupinus diffusus*)

The stems of lupine, with 2- to 5-inch-long hairy, oval leaves, lie sprawling along the ground. Upright stalks bear numerous two-lipped blue flowers with a conspicuous white or cream spot on the large upper lip, or standard. This white spot distinguishes it from the few other species found in the Southeast. Many more species of lupine are found in the West, including the famed Texas bluebonnet. Lupines have been hybridized to produce even more spectacular garden plants.

The name lupine comes from the Latin *lupus*, meaning wolf. The plants were believed to deplete the soil, "wolfing" up all the nutrients. In fact lupines, like all members of the bean family, enrich the soil with nitrogen through the action of bacteria living in nodules on their roots.

Sandhill rosemary
(*Ceratiola ericoides*)

Found in deep white sands on the driest sandhills, ridges, and dunes, sandhill rosemary is an evergreen shrub that indeed looks and smells like the herb rosemary. Growing to 10 feet tall, sandhill rosemary has narrow needlelike leaves. Male and female flowers are found on separate plants, near the tips of young branches, on the stem between the leaves. The flowers are so small that a hand lens or magnifying glass is needed to see the details. Two rounded anthers on the male or two threadlike styles on the female extend beyond a ring of two tiny petals and two tiny red or yellow sepals.

In the areas where sandhill rosemary grows, only a few other widely scattered plants can survive. It has adapted to the occurrence of natural wildfires every 10 to 40 years: it is not a long-lived plant and only produces seeds between the ages of about 10 to 35 years. Moreover, the seeds need fire to germinate. More frequent lightning fires are unlikely, because plant litter accumulates very slowly in these barren areas.

star, annual balduina, grass-leaved golden-aster, St. Andrew's cross, and bush goldenrod.

The road comes to a Y—the short arm to the left is used mostly for parking, and the arm to the right is the walking trail through the Ohoopee Dunes. As you move out onto the dunes, the area opens up, with more shrubs and a ground cover of little round balls of reindeer lichen. The rare sandhill rosemary will be in bloom in spring. To distinguish the male shrubs from the female shrubs, get up close and look at the differences in the tiny flowers,

Bush goldenrod
(*Chrysoma pauciflosculosa*)

Resembling goldenrod, with masses of small yellow flowers, bush goldenrod brightens sandhills and dunes in late summer and fall. It is a multibranched shrub with narrow oblong leaves crowded near the ends of the branches. In summer some of the branches grow rapidly and produce clusters of flowers on the new growth. After the seeds have been produced, the new stems die back to the woody branches, which remain over winter.

Although bush goldenrod historically has been grouped in the same genus as goldenrods, botanists now place it in a separate genus.

Red basil
(*Clinopodium coccineum*, synonyms *Satureja coccinea*, *Calamintha coccinea*)

Along with bush goldenrod, red basil adds color to the sandhills and dry pine barrens in summer and fall. It is a small shrub that grows to about 3 feet. A member of the mint family, it is also known as scarlet calamint. Red, or sometimes yellow, tubular flowers more than an inch long have a prominent lower lip, with a shorter triangular upper lip and lateral lobes.

Other members of the genus grow in dry areas of the Southeast, but these all have pink to lavender (rarely white) flowers. One of these, Ohoopee Dunes wild basil, is found only on the dunes along the Ohoopee River and some 200 miles farther south on the Lake Wales Sand Ridge in Florida. It is considered threatened in both states.

located between the narrow leaves. Males have two rounded anthers, while females have two threadlike pistils. Near the end of this leg of the walk, **lupine** flowers in bunches near the trail. This area will be lit up by **bush goldenrod** in late summer and early fall. Another **Chickasaw plum** is on the left where the trail meets Hall's Bridge Road. Turn right (west) and return to the starting point. Many of the flowers found along the first part of the walk can also be found along Hall's Bridge Road. It is especially nice in spring, when a large number of **lupines** are flowering.

You should also notice the damage off-road vehicles have done to the environment on the south side of the road. So far, they have not torn up the protected natural area on the north side of Hall's Bridge Road.

17
River Bluff Trail
Montezuma Bluffs Natural Area

Flowering Season	March through May
Peak Flowering	Mid-March to Mid-April
Walk Length	Less than 0.5 mile
Walk Rating	Easy
Restrooms	None
Fee	None

Directions

From Montezuma take Ga. 49 north from its intersection with Ga. 26 for 3.3 miles. Turn left on Crooks Landing Road. Soon the road descends steeply down a bluff. Take the first right turn, into a parking area with a kiosk. The walk starts at the kiosk.

Environment

The walk follows a flat terrace on a rare Coastal Plain limestone bluff located along the Flint River. In this mixed hardwood forest, the trees are **American beech**, **southern magnolia**, **American hornbeam**, **spruce pine**, **eastern hophornbeam**, and **southern red oak**. What makes the area unusual is not the diversity of its vegetation, but the profuse flowering of the unusual plants that grow here. In particular, the ravines provide a cool refuge for the rare and endangered **relict trillium**.

The Walk

The initial part of the walk passes through a weedy patch with plants such as **lyre-leaved sage**, **Carolina cranesbill**, and an exotic, **periwinkle**. **Yellow jasmine** climbs in the trees, and in late spring **Japanese privet** flowers. But the trail soon enters the forest, where one immediately finds **needle palm**, identified by the sharp needles around the base of the plant. There are **cutleaf toothworts** by the zillions. Here and there are patches of **blue phlox**. A short spur leads to an overlook with a view of the floodplain below, brightened by the yellow

blooms of **ragwort**. Along the path are **mottled trillium** and **relict trillium**. One may still see the distinctive kidney-shaped, lobed leaves of **bloodroot**, but the flowers fade early in March. To find the flowers of **heart-leaf**, look for little brown jugs under low clumps of shiny, mottled heart-shaped leaves. The incongruously named **white blue-eyed-grass**, a member of the iris family, appears here and there. Like several other blue-eyed grasses, it is not blue at all, but white to pale violet. A number of **buttercups** are blooming, but they are difficult to identify to species. Also found here is an exotic, **bedstraw**. The trail makes a turn and loops back to the main path near the overlook spur, to return to the parking area.

By late spring, when the deciduous trees shade the forest floor, most of the spring flowers have gone. But the bright blue of **hairyflower spiderwort** continues to brighten the forest floor for a few more weeks.

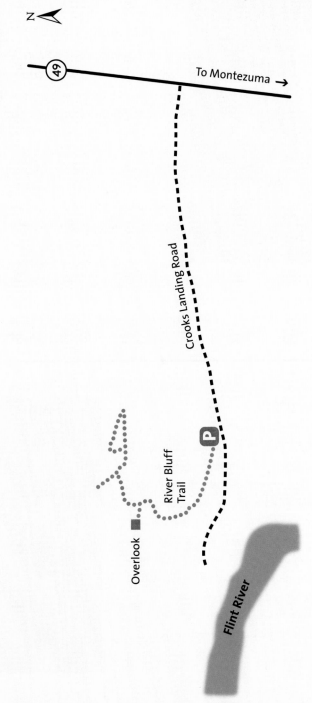

RIVER BLUFF TRAIL
MONTEZUMA BLUFFS
NATURAL AREA

N

49

To Montezuma →

Crooks Landing Road

P

River Bluff
Trail

Overlook

Flint River

Cutleaf toothwort
(*Cardamine concatenata*, synonym *Dentaria laciniata*)

In moist, rich hardwood forests, this species of toothwort spreads its clusters of pinkish-white bells for a few weeks each spring. Each little bell has four equal petals joined to form a tube near the base. The stem usually has three leaves, divided into three or five leaflets. The seeds form in long, narrow upright pods that snap open when ripe, casting the seeds several feet from the mother plant. The rhizomes of some species have toothlike projections, hence the name toothwort.

Toothworts belong to the mustard family. Their tubers (enlarged underground stems) have a peppery taste and can be ground and used like horseradish. Native tribes of the eastern United States used the roots and tubers to treat toothache and stomach ailments.

Blue phlox
(*Phlox divaricata*)

An uncommon plant found in deciduous woodlands, blue phlox can produce a swath of blue to lavender flower clusters to enhance the spring display. *Divaricata* means spreading, referring to the way new shoots radiate from the plant like spokes of a wheel. These stems can root at the nodes to form new plants, so that a wide-spreading colony results.

Each flower has a narrow tube broadening into a flat whorl of five ▸▸

petals at the end. The flowers are fragrant, like those of most phloxes, so they are often called sweet Williams. The center may be white, blue, or magenta. A few pairs of oval leaves are spread along the stem. Both leaves and stems are hairy.

Heart-leaf (*Hexastylis arifolia*)

The mottled evergreen leaves of heart-leaf are showier than its flowers. They are often shaped more like an arrowhead than a heart, and they arise from an underground stem, making low clumps that enlarge only slowly, adding one or a few leaves each year. The inconspicuous flowers are tucked underneath the leaves and have no petals. Instead, the sepals are joined into a flask-shaped structure with three flaring lobes above a narrow neck. Inside are twelve stamens and six styles, hence the genus name from the Greek *hexa* (six) and *stylis* (styles). Usually brownish-pink in color, they are also called little brown jugs and are fun to discover by lifting up the leaves in early spring. The flowers are pollinated by low-flying insects such as gnats and carrion flies.

Relict trillium (*Trillium reliquum*)

Relict trillium is another of the purple-flowered toadshades. It differs from mottled trillium in that it has a curving stem, so that the flower lies close to the ground. Its erect petals are less than half as long as the leaves and are slightly twisted. The leaves are mottled in at least five shades, from silvery green to a deep blue-green. Enclosed by the petals, the stamens have prominent beaks on their tips. (Those of mottled trillium are hardly beaked at all.)

Not recognized as a new species until 1975, relict trillium is found at only about thirty widely scattered and relatively undisturbed sites, most in Georgia. They are believed to be relicts, remnants of a once widespread population, from glacial times, when North America was cooler, although there were no glaciers this far south. The species is federally protected.

Mottled trillium
(*Trillium maculatum*)

Mottled trillium, a fairly common trillium of moist woodlands of the Coastal Plain, has three long, narrow, maroon petals with a noticeable narrowing at the base. They are slightly spreading, so that the interior of the flower can be seen from the side. The top sides of the much shorter sepals are tinged with maroon or striped in green and maroon. The three leaves have a strong variegation, but with just two or three shades of green. The flower sits just atop the leaves with no stalk, and flower and leaves are held on an upright stem.

Many of the trillium species in which the flowers are stalkless are called toadshades because of their mottled or variegated leaves. They are difficult to tell apart. Most have foul-smelling, maroon-petaled flowers, with occasional yellow or greenish individuals.

18
Ann Barber Wildflower Trail
Doerun Pitcherplant Bog Natural Area

Flowering Season	March through October
Peak Flowering	April and May, August and September
Walk Length	About 1 mile
Walk Rating	Easy level walking. In wet seasons parts of the trail are underwater. Be prepared to get your feet wet.
Restrooms	None
Fee	None

Directions From Moultrie take Ga. 133 northwest about 9 miles. Look for a wooden sign identifying the natural area on the right side of the road. Turn right on the gravel access road, which drops rather steeply from the highway, and drive about 100 yards to a parking area and information kiosk.

Environment The walk makes a double loop through a longleaf pine–wiregrass community with three concentrated pitcher-plant bogs. At the time of the first European settlement, there were more than 90 million acres of longleaf pine–wiregrass habitat in the southeastern Coastal Plain from Virginia to East Texas, including the northern two-thirds of Florida. In Georgia and Alabama the habitat extended into the Piedmont and the Ridge and Valley regions. Forestry practices, clearing for agriculture, and fire suppression have left only a tiny fraction of the original forest.

Longleaf pine is adapted to the frequent lightning fires that these habitats experience. During the tree's early development, the bud is protected by a compact arrangement of needles. This stage lasts for a number of years. In fact, one of the challenges for commercial plantation of **longleaf pine** is the length of time the trees need to develop to harvestable size.

Thus **longleaf pine** areas were reseeded with faster-growing **slash pine** or **loblolly pine**. **Wiregrass** provides the fuel for periodic burns, which it needs in order to reproduce and thus to survive. Without fire, hardwood trees would eventually shade out the **wiregrass** and compete with the **longleaf pines** for light, space, and nutrients.

The underlying rock is limestone, overlain by sandy soils. In places, a hardpan does not allow water to drain well. Bogs, often containing pitcher-plants, develop where soils become water-logged and poorly aerated during the rainy season (Mitchell 1999). The pitcher-plant bogs, too, need periodic fires. Without them, shrubs take over and outcompete the pitcher-plants. At Doerun, the Department of Natural Resources conducts periodic prescribed burns to maintain the habitat. The timing and amount of flowering are affected by the timing and severity of the burns.

We consider the Ann Barber Wildflower Trail the premier wildflower walk in the Coastal Plain. As Charles Wharton (1978) wrote, "Esthetically, this is one of South Georgia's most beautiful environments. The floral displays (including those of rare lilies and orchids) are both extensive and sequential, from early spring through fall."

The Walk   Because the area is burned frequently, it is difficult to mark the trail permanently. By midsummer, rampant growth tends to obscure the path. However, you can see the parking area from all parts of the trail, so it is impossible to get lost. (It would still be a good idea to carry the trail map with you.) The walk begins to the left of the kiosk. Within a few yards (point **A**) a spur goes left to the deck overlooking Bog 1. From the deck return to point **A** and turn left toward the little bridge crossing a small drainage (point **B**). The trail curves left until it reaches point **C**. Here it is usually necessary to detour to the right around Bog 2, which is generally knee-deep in mud and water. At point **D** a visible path goes left across the bog. Once across (point **E**), look for a path to the left, which makes a clockwise loop through a drier area. The loop reaches an old dirt road and follows it a short distance before heading back to point **E**. From here go back across the bog to point **D**, then continue straight to point **F**, where another small bridge crosses the drainage. Immediately across the bridge, the trail turns left and then curves right to reach Bog 3. The path then angles toward the entry road and follows alongside it a short way to the parking area.

In spring **bird-foot violet**, **sunbonnets**, **Coastal Plain blue-eyed-grass**, and **yellow star-grass** bloom beside the short path to the boardwalk overlooking Bog 1. In the bogs **yellow pitcher-plants** make a spectacular display. All three bogs have **yellow pitcher-plants**; the third one has **hooded pitcher-plants** as well.

In spring flowers bloom all along the trail. Look for **pine-**

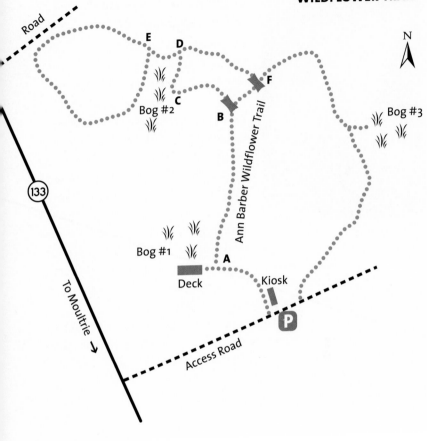

land wild-indigo with conspicuous yellow flowers, **tread-softly,**
spring helenium, white-top fleabane, trailing bluet, hairy-
flower spiderwort, hatpins, and **bog buttons. Hatpins** and **bog**
buttons are difficult to distinguish from one another because
both look like little white buttons on a long stem. A low, shrubby
St. John's-wort will also be in flower.

By late spring the list of flowers is even more extensive. Little
pencil-flower has yellow flowers of the familiar bean family type.

Smooth meadow-beauty (*Rhexia alifanus*)

The flowers and fruit of smooth meadow-beauty add their charm to moist pinelands, savannas, and ditches of the Coastal Plain from North Carolina to Texas. The distinctive flower has four spreading, asymmetrical lavender or rose petals that look rather like fan blades. The eight anthers, bearing yellow pollen, are attached at right angles to their filaments, forming a "knee." The petals are attached to the edge of a reddish, hairy, urn-shaped receptacle that holds the ovary and later the fruit. *Alifanus*, which means "little earthen cup," refers to this receptacle, which persists conspicuously after the petals have fallen. The smooth, 3-foot-tall stems have pairs of blue-green, lance-shaped leaves, angled upward.

Meadow-beauties belong to the melastome family, which has about four thousand species, mostly in the tropics of the Western Hemisphere. But the thirteen or so species of meadow-beauty grow almost entirely in the continental United States.

Several milkworts can be found, especially in the dry area on the far side of the second bog: **bachelor's button** is yellow, as is **short milkwort**, but **candyweed** is orange, even though the species name, *lutea*, means yellow. With a similar name, but not related to the milkworts, **Michaux's milkweed** blooms on the first leg of the trail and elsewhere. **Star-grass**, **queen's-delight**, and **blackroot** will most likely be found along the farthest loop on the other side of the second bog. The delicate light blue blossoms of **Small's skullcap** and the striking white flowers of **pawpaw** are likely to be found near the parking area on both the first and last sections

Short milkwort
(*Polygala ramosa*)

The yellow flowers of the short milkwort bloom on branching stems that resemble candelabra, the whole plant reaching to about 1 foot tall. Milkworts' intricate flowers include five sepals, three small ones and two large lateral ones, called wings, the same color as the petals. The three petals are fused into a flaring tube that is usually fringed at the end. In most milkworts the flowers are small and packed tightly into spikes or racemes, so that the parts are difficult to see.

Polygala is from the Greek *polugalon*, which means "much milk." An old belief held that feeding milkworts to cattle would increase their milk production.

Yellow pitcher-plant
(*Sarracenia flava*)

With their stiff, hollow leaves of yellow or green, sometimes veined and splotched with red, and their large, drooping yellow flowers, yellow pitcher-plants are hard to miss. The flowers are borne singly on an arching stem so that they hang downward. The five sepals and five long yellow petals enclose the pistil, which is broadened at the end into a stiff platform resembling an upside-down umbrella. The platform serves as a resting place for bees and other pollinators, trapping falling pollen that may then adhere to their bodies.

The wet, strongly acidic soils of bogs are deficient in nutrients, particularly nitrogen, so the pitcher-plant's hollow leaves are adapted to catch and digest insects. Insects flying or falling into the tubular leaves are prevented from climbing out by downward-projecting hairs and drown in the fluids that collect at the bottom of the leaves.

In former years, colonies of yellow pitcher-plants were conspicuous in wet areas throughout the Coastal Plain, but habitat loss has significantly reduced their numbers. Collectors have also depleted pitcher-plant communities, but there is really no reason to dig them up: they are easily propagated from seed and quite available inexpensively through the nursery trade.

Hooded pitcher-plant (*Sarracenia minor*)

This pitcher-plant's flowers are smaller and paler than those of yellow pitcher-plant, and their stalks are shorter. The hooded pitcher-plant's hollow leaves are reddish green, with white translucent spots on the back opposite the opening, and have a hood that arches over the opening. Because the hood shields the opening, insects do not fall in and drown. Instead a trail of nectar entices them to enter. Like moths at a streetlight, they try to escape through the translucent openings and eventually exhaust themselves, falling to the bottom, where they are digested.

Hooded pitcher-plant is the most common pitcher-plant of bogs and low pinelands of the Coastal Plain from North Carolina to Florida.

of the trail. All along the walk, **dyschoriste** is hidden low among the vegetation, while the flower of **rose-rush** sways in the breezes on slender wands three feet high.

New species flower in summer. Among them are **green milkweed**, **elephant's-foot**, **common ten-angled pipewort**, **ironweed**,

Comfort-root
(*Hibiscus aculeatus*)

The large, five-petaled, creamy white flowers of comfort-root, stained crimson to dark purple near their centers, are hard to overlook. Comfort-root has the unusual flower structure of the mallow family to which it belongs. The numerous stamens are fused into a long tube, or column, with the pollen-bearing anthers emerging from its sides. The five-parted pistil extends through the opening at the end of the column. As the flower ages, the petals turn yellow and then pink.

Comfort-root is found in pine savannas and flatwoods of the Coastal Plain from North Carolina to Louisiana. The arching stems are 3 to 4 feet long, the leaves are palmately divided into three or five lobes, and both stems and leaves have very rough hairs. The flowers appear singly in the upper leaf axils from June to August. Other members of the mallow family include cotton, okra, and hollyhocks.

St. Andrew's cross, carphephorus, smooth meadow-beauty, yellow-eyed-grass, galactia, rattlebox, and milkworts such as **Curtiss's milkwort, drum-heads,** and **candyweed.** The list goes on: **grassleaf blazing-star, rayless goldenrod, hyptis,** and **gerardia.**

Three conspicuous plants, each found in only one spot near the trail, stand out as late summer gems: bright orange-red **pine lily, comfort-root,** and **gopher apple,** the last in fruit.

The flowering season winds down somewhat in fall, but **rayless sunflower, blue sage, senna seymeria,** and **savanna cowbane** bloom on the first part of the walk.

19
Swamp Island Drive and Swamp Walk
Okefenokee National Wildlife Refuge

Flowering Season	March through October
Peak Flowering	Mid-April to Mid-May
Walk Length	2 or more miles, depending on walks taken
Walk Rating	Easy, flat walks
Restrooms	At Visitor Center and at boardwalk parking lot
Fee	Entrance fee

Directions From Folkston drive south on Ga. 121 for 8 miles to the main entrance road. Turn right (west) and drive 5 miles to the Visitor Center. The turnoff to Swamp Island Drive is on the left just before the Visitor Center.

Environment Okefenokee is a depression swamp. Although it is mainly a peat bog, it includes a number of other habitats. To the east, Trail Ridge, a former barrier island created millions of years ago, blocks drainage directly to the Atlantic. A man-made 4.5-mile-long sill prevents excess drainage to the west. Two rivers drain the swamp: the St. Marys River drains to the southeast; the Suwannee River drains to the southwest.

Second in extent to the peat bogs are forests of **pond-cypress**: together the bogs and cypress forests comprise more than half the refuge. On the slightly higher ground of islands, pine barrens and some hardwood hammocks are found. Other habitats include open water (lakes), gum or bay forests, and prairies. The prairies are really shallow lakes, 1 to 3 feet deep, filled with floating and emergent plants such as white **water-lilies** and **golden-club**, and crisscrossed with alligator runs and canoe and boat trails. The lake bottom is a brownish peat that is stirred up by outboard motors and clogs their intakes.

Swamp Island Drive passes mostly through pine flatlands typical of the southeastern Coastal Plain. It crosses two hard-

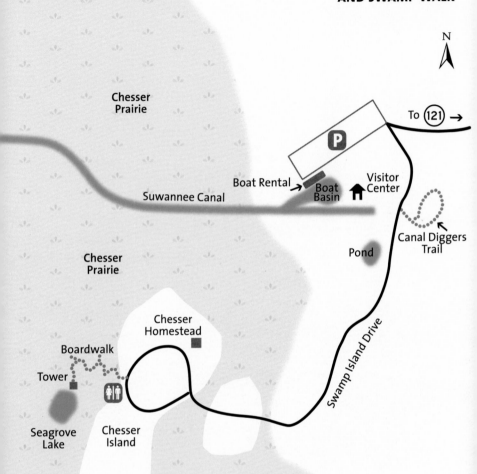

SWAMP ISLAND DRIVE AND SWAMP WALK

N

Chesser
Prairie

To (121) →

P

Boat Rental →

Boat
Basin

Visitor
Center

Suwannee Canal

Canal Diggers
Trail

Chesser
Prairie

Pond

Chesser
Homestead

Boardwalk

Swamp Island Drive

Tower

Seagrove
Lake

Chesser
Island

Water-lily
(*Nymphaea odorata*)

In the shallow sunlit prairies, the water-lily's leaves and flowers float on the surface, while its thick rhizome anchors it to the bottom. The fragrant flowers have many rings of pointed white (occasionally pink) petals and golden yellow centers. The large oval leaves lie flat on the water and have a distinctive cleft where the stem attaches. The flower opens in late morning and closes in the evening. After three or four days, the flower closes permanently, and its stem contracts in a spiral, pulling the fruit down near the bottom, where the seeds mature.

A common plant of shallow freshwater in the eastern and mid-western United States, water-lily often forms dense stands. Its leaves, buds, and seeds can be eaten, and its root has been used in treating diarrhea and rashes.

wood hammocks: the Canal Diggers Trail enters one, and the Chesser Homestead was built in another. The boardwalk to Owl's Roost Tower passes through cypress, gum, and bay forests and prairies, and finally to a view of the open water of Seagrove Lake.

The Walk From the Visitor Center parking area, drive back toward the entrance. Take the first right turn onto Swamp Island Drive. The first stop is the Canal Diggers Trail to your left. In the 1890s, the Suwannee Canal was dug in an attempt to drain the swamp to the east. It was a failure: water flowed the other way! Here a short walk in spring yields the white blossoms of **stagger-bush**, **wax myrtle**, **evergreen blueberry**, and **tread-softly**. An orchid, **rose pogonia**, and **pawpaw**, with its creamy, floppy flowers, bloom on this trail.

Return to the car and drive on to a large pond on the right, often occupied by an alligator or two. Around the pond in spring, look for the orange flowers of **candyweed**. Across the road is a grove of pines in which red-cockaded woodpeckers have made nest holes.

A ditch on the left, a little further along the road, is occupied by a big female alligator, sometimes with little gators. Beware not only of alligators but of snakes that may be hiding in the grasses beside the ditches. Nonetheless, **floating bladderwort** makes a beautiful yellow swath in the ditch, mirrored by the black tannic water. On the left just before the ditch, look for tall, white, open clusters of **crow-poison**. On the right about 20 yards beyond the ditch, the rare **hartwrightia** shows its pale lavender flowers in fall. Also visible beside the road in fall is **threadleaf false-foxglove**. Further along the road, yellow **colicroot** blooms in spring.

After a short distance, there is another long borrow ditch on the left side of the road. We once saw a black bear here early in the morning. This is a wonderful spot for wildflowers. In spring **hooded** and **parrot pitcher-plants**, **rose pogonia**, **grass-pink**, and **water-lilies** are some of the beauties blooming here, while on the opposite side of the road, **violet butterworts** flower.

Next the drive begins a one-way loop to the right, passing Chesser Homestead, which is worth a stop, although for its history, not its wildflowers. After the homestead you will see the parking lot for the boardwalk to Owl's Roost Tower (1.5 miles round-trip). The walk quickly enters a **blackgum** forest, where you will soon encounter a vine with a fascinating growth habit. **Climbing fetter-bush** blooms in early spring with white, bell-shaped flowers. On the ground it only grows to about 3 feet high, but if it can find a **pond-cypress** nearby, it climbs 30 or 40 feet up in the furrows of the bark. The bark grows around the **climbing fetter-bush** stem, hiding it from view, so that the branches of the **climbing fetter-bush** appear to be branches of the cypress (except that their leaves are entirely wrong for cypress). The **climbing fetter-bush** does not seem to injure the cypress tree.

The boardwalk passes into a bay forest with many **loblolly-bays**, which bloom with beautiful white flowers in late summer. In this area many golden silk spiders spin their impressive webs from late summer into fall. Then comes a view of prairies and open water where, in early spring, **golden-club** flowers. Spring brings **hooded pitcher-plants** and **yellow pitcher-plants**, as well as some that look like hybrids of the two. In late spring, **white arum** flowers here. As one might expect, the prairie is abloom in summer, with **redroot, yellow-eyed-grass, titi**, and **pipewort**. Then in fall come **tickseed sunflower** and **bur-marigold**.

Moving on into more loblolly–bay forest and then quickly into a cypress forest, the boardwalk ends at the 50-foot Owl's Roost Tower. The view from the top reveals the extent of Okefenokee

Golden-club
(*Orontium aquaticum*)

Sharing the prairies with the water-lilies, golden-club crowds hundreds of tiny yellow flowers onto the top of an elongated clublike structure called a spadix. The white spadix rises a foot or more above the water. The blue-green leaves are narrow ovals, somewhat shorter than the spadix, and can be upright or prone on the water surface. Because they are coated with a thick wax, the leaves shed water instantly after being moistened, leading to another common name, never-wet.

The plant contains tiny crystals of calcium oxalate in all its tissues and if eaten raw can cause severe irritation and swelling of the mouth and throat. But by boiling and thoroughly drying the roots and seeds, Native Americans were able to eat them.

Rose pogonia
(*Pogonia ophioglossoides*)

Rose pogonia is a lovely pink orchid of
swamps, bogs, and wet habitats of the
Coastal Plain. *Pogon* means "beard" and
refers to the three rows of bristly hairs
along the midline of the lower petal. The
flower has three sepals and three petals.
The two upper petals, narrow ovals,
resemble the three sepals. The lower petal,
or lip, is broader and elaborately fringed
on its edges. The flowering stem bears
only one flower and has an oval leaf about
4 inches long midway up the stem.

Floating bladderwort
(*Utricularia inflata*)

The ingenious carnivorous lifestyle of
floating bladderwort provides it with
nutrients not available from the water in
which it floats. The plant is completely
unanchored. A whorl of leaves with
hollow, inflated stalks and midribs
supports a stem with several small yellow
flowers. Below the surface is a network
of narrow leaves and stems bearing tiny
bladders that can open quickly, sucking
in microscopic animals that brush against
them. Enzymes digest the captive.

In winter only the submerged parts
of the plant remain. In spring the whorl of flotation leaves and the
flowering stalk begin to develop underwater, and when these parts have
become sufficiently buoyant, they pop to the surface. In drought the
plant forms tubers that remain in the soil until the wetland is again filled
with water, when they produce new plants.

Parrot pitcher-plant (*Sarracenia psittacina*)

The parrot pitcher-plant's dark crimson flowers on foot-long stalks appear in spring and are much more conspicuous than the pitchers. These tubular leaves form a rosette that lies on the ground often hidden by grasses and other vegetation. The hood at the tip of each leaf turns upward, almost covering the opening but leaving a small space at each side where insects can enter the tube. The pitcher thus resembles a parrot's beak.

Parrot pitcher-plants grow in peat bogs, wet savannas, and along ditches and swales in open pinelands. These are places where water levels fluctuate, sometimes submerging the leaves. By lying horizontal, the leaves may be able to capture small waterborne creatures when submerged, as well flying insects during drier periods.

National Wildlife Refuge. Directly in front is Seagrove Lake. Often an alligator or two can be spied moving across it. Sometimes one can spot sandhill cranes, as well as herons and egrets. The tops of the cypress trees are close to the tower, so examine the needles for the identifying characteristics of the **pond-cypress**: they are awl shaped and appressed along ascending branchlets.

On the return to the parking lot, take time to look for alligator runs and holes. There is usually one at the beginning of the prairie and another back in the **blackgum** forest. For a different and more intimate view of the Okefenokee, rent a canoe from the concessionaire near the Visitor Center and paddle into Chesser Prairie. Tour boats into Chesser Prairie can also provide a fine experience, but the noise of the motor does detract from the ambiance.

20

Clam Creek Bicycle Path, Glory Path, and St. Andrews Picnic Area

Jekyll Island

Flowering Season	April through October
Peak Flowering	April and May
Walk Length	Three walks totaling 2 miles
Walk Rating	Easy
Restrooms	Clam Creek Picnic Area and St. Andrews Picnic Area
Fee	Entrance fee

Directions From Brunswick take Ga. 520 east to Jekyll Island. Pay fee at entrance and continue straight on Ben Fortson Parkway to Beachview Drive. Turn left (north) on Beachview Drive, go about 4.5 miles, turn right (north) to Clam Creek Picnic Area, and park in the lot by the fishing pier.

Environment Jekyll Island is one of Georgia's fifteen barrier islands. Of the four islands with causeways to the mainland, Jekyll is the only one that is publicly owned, and it has by far the largest preserved natural area, about two-thirds of the island. Most of Jekyll is a state-owned resort, while the other three, Tybee, St. Simons, and Sea Island, are privately owned residential and recreational areas. Of the remaining islands, four are privately owned, Cumberland is a national seashore, and the rest are controlled by Georgia or the federal government as wildlife refuges, preserves, or research areas. The natural habitats and flora of all the barrier islands are similar. While not rich in wildflower species, these islands host distinct vegetation adapted to salt, sand, and wind. About 7 miles long by 1.5 miles wide, Jekyll is one of the smaller barrier islands but contains all of the major island habitats: ocean beach and dunes, salt marsh, maritime forest, and freshwater ponds and sloughs.

Jekyll, like many of Georgia's barrier islands, was purchased

in the late nineteenth century by some of the nation's wealthiest families, who used it as a winter retreat. It was spared the rapid development that overtook some islands and was purchased as a park site by the state in 1947. For the next two years it was operated as a state park. In 1950 the island was turned over to the Jekyll Island Authority to manage it on behalf of the state. The board of the Jekyll Island Authority is appointed by the governor.

The Walks

Clam Creek Bicycle Path: This path begins at the parking area for the fishing pier, crosses a footbridge over Clam Creek, then turns to the right (south) and traverses a salt marsh. As it nears Beachview Drive, a sandy path to the left leads to Driftwood Beach. The bicycle path then turns right to reach Beachview Drive. You can return by the same route, follow the road back to the parking area, or take the path to Driftwood Beach and (tide permitting) return along the beach to Clam Creek. Clam Creek is a fine example of the salt marsh habitat that extends between the barrier islands and the mainland in a band 2 to 6 miles wide from St. Marys north to Savannah, an area of 393,000 acres, of which 286,000 acres is **smooth cordgrass. Smooth cordgrass** fills the center of the tidal marsh at Clam Creek. It outcompetes other plants here because it is better adapted to handle the saltwater. Around the edges of the marsh, on slightly higher ground that does not receive the incoming tides as frequently, grow plants that are somewhat less salt tolerant than **smooth cordgrass**: **black rush**, and still higher, **sea ox-eye**.

In spring **shepherd's needle, seaside pennywort** with its nearly round leaves, and **trailing bluets** flower on the left side of the path. **Three-seeded mercury** flowers in fall at this location. Along the asphalt path as it curves south, two shrubs, **yaupon**

Sea ox-eye (*Borrichia frutescens*)

Sea ox-eye's composite flower heads resemble those of daisies, formed from two types of flowers. The disc flowers are somewhat tubular and are packed into the center, while the yellow ray flowers form the ring of "petals" on the edge. The flower heads form at the tips of the mostly unbranched stems and may bloom from May to September. The dark, spiny bracts of the disc flowers remain on the plant through the winter.

Like many seaside plants, sea ox-eye is adapted to withstand brackish water. It is a low-growing woody plant with somewhat succulent stems and leaves, and it spreads by underground stems to form large patches. It is common on the Coastal Plain from Virginia to Florida and west to Texas.

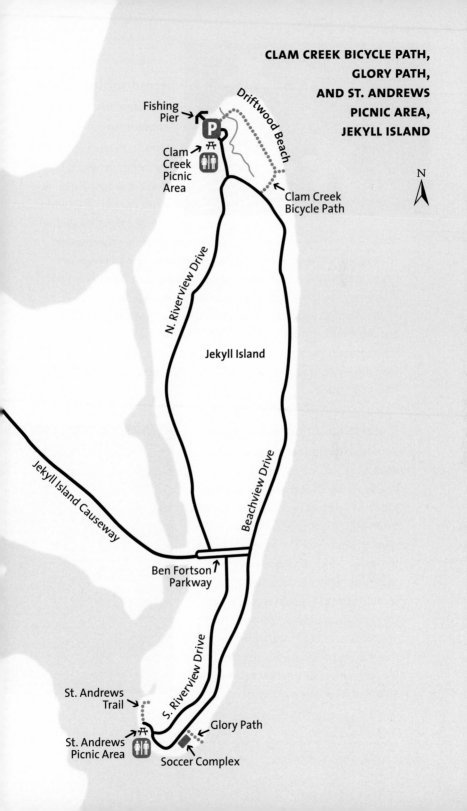

CLAM CREEK BICYCLE PATH,
GLORY PATH,
AND ST. ANDREWS
PICNIC AREA,
JEKYLL ISLAND

N

Fishing
Pier

Driftwood Beach

Clam
Creek
Picnic
Area

Clam Creek
Bicycle Path

N. Riverview Drive

Jekyll Island

Beachview Drive

Jekyll Island Causeway

Ben Fortson
Parkway

S. Riverview Drive

St. Andrews
Trail

Glory Path

St. Andrews
Picnic Area

Soccer Complex

Tread-softly (*Cnidoscolus stimulosus*)

Other common names for this plant include bull-nettle and mala mujer ("bad woman" in Spanish), warning that tread-softly should be seen but not touched. Its leaves and stems are covered with stinging hairs that are painful on contact and may cause a severe rash. Found in sunny areas with dry, sandy soils throughout the Coastal Plain, it is usually low growing but can reach a height of 3 feet.

In spite of its armor, it is a rather pretty plant. The leaves are lobed and resemble hairy oak leaves. Flowers are either male, bearing pollen, or female, producing seeds. There are no true petals, but the male flowers have five white petal-like sepals, while the inconspicuous female flowers have tiny sepals.

Coral bean (*Erythrina herbacea*)

Coral bean can be found in thin woods with sandy soils, often adjacent to beaches or dunes. It may grow as tall as 5 feet in Florida, but in Georgia it dies back in the winter and therefore is shorter. Its spires of bright red flowers appear before the leaves, which are divided into three triangular segments. After flowering, pods containing equally bright scarlet seeds may remain on the plant for some time. The seeds have been used for jewelry, but they may be poisonous if eaten. This is the only temperate member of the genus *Erythrina*. All others are tropical.

Galactia
(*Galactia elliottii*)

Galactia is a weak vine that in some cases climbs by twining around nearby objects and in others simply sprawls along the ground. Most galactias have compound leaves divided into three leaflets. This species is the only one with five to nine segments. Its flower is a typical pea flower with a large upper petal, or standard; two lateral petals; and two lower petals joined to form a boat-shaped keel. The flowers are white, occasionally tinged with red, and appear from July to September in sandy, open woodlands. The name *galactia* comes from the Greek work for "milky" and stems from an error by the Englishman, Patrick Browne, who named the genus, mistakenly believing the plants had milky sap.

and **wax myrtle**, flower in spring. The leaves of **yaupon** contain caffeine and were used by Native Americans to prepare a ceremonial emetic drink. In fall the berries of **yaupon** are bright red; those of **wax myrtle** are a waxy grayish-blue and have been used in candle making. Also in fall, **groundsel tree** and **false willow** bear male and female flowers on separate plants. The numerous white hairy bristles of the female flowers give the whole plant a cottony appearance. The perennial **saltmarsh aster** flowers at this time too.

On higher ground surrounding the marsh is a maritime strand forest, dominated by **live oak**, **eastern redcedar**, and **cabbage palmetto**. The **live oak** branches are draped with **Spanish-moss**, which gives the forest a mysterious, almost tropical feeling. **Cross-vine** climbs in the trees. In the dark and less breezy inte-

Sea-rocket
(*Cakile edentula*)

The common name comes from the unusual shape of the fruit. It is divided into two parts: the part closest to the stem has only one or sometimes no seed, while the outer part narrows to a short beak and contains one seed. The outer part becomes corky before breaking off and can float away to disperse the seed. The inner part remains on the plant and drops its seed nearby. Flowers, at the ends of branches, have four white or pink petals.

Sea-rocket is a widespread species, occurring along the Atlantic Coast from Newfoundland to Florida and along the Gulf Coast to Texas. Its succulent leaves and stems make it quite tolerant of saltwater, so that it thrives on the upper beaches and outermost dunes. Stems and leaves have been widely used in salads and are said to have a mild horseradish flavor.

rior of the forest, there is very little herb layer. An active population of gnats and mosquitoes makes standing still to photograph a plant distinctly uncomfortable.

From the bicycle path, where it nears Beachview Drive, turn left on a sandy path and walk to Driftwood Beach. This is a fabulous place to photograph the sunrise and to witness the erosion occurring along these barrier islands. Typically sand from the northern ends of the islands is moved southward by longshore currents, which deposit the sand on the southern ends as beach additions and sand spits. Dredging to keep the sound just north of Jekyll open for shipping interrupts the movement of sand from St. Simons Island toward Jekyll, accelerating the erosion of the north end of Jekyll (Schoettle 1996). The beach is retreating into the maritime forest, resulting in a fantastic and eerie boneyard of dead **live oaks** with twisted shapes out of Dr. Seuss.

Glory Path: Drive south on Beachview Drive about 2 miles past Ben Fortson Parkway to the soccer field complex on the 4-H property. Drive through the gate to the parking lot on the far side of the soccer fields. A boardwalk, constructed to provide beach access for actors and equipment during the filming of the movie *Glory*, crosses the dunes to the beach, passing through shrub thickets and dune meadows. In fall **camphorweed** and **grass-leaved golden-aster** flower in the dune meadows, while out on the primary dunes adjacent to the beach, **beach-tea**, **sea-rocket**, and **fiddle-leaf morning-glory** bloom. On these first dunes, look for **sea-oats**, whose leaves, buried stems, and roots help stabilize the dunes and prevent drifting.

St. Andrews Picnic Area: Drive to the end of Beachview Drive, which goes straight into the picnic area parking lot. **Resurrection fern**, **Spanish-moss**, and **ball moss**, a threatened plant in Georgia, grow on the limbs of huge **live oaks** in the picnic area. Beneath the trees off to the right, between the picnic area and a tidal marsh, **tread-softly**, **trailing bluet**, **Georgia frostweed**, **galactia**, **Ohio spiderwort**, and **coral bean** flower in spring. The beach at St. Andrews provides a grand view of the sunset over the mainland.

Appendix

SUMMARY OF WALKS BY FLOWERING SEASON

Walk

Shirley Miller Wildflower Trail

Cedar Glade Walks

Keown Falls Trail

Pocket Recreation Area Interpretive Trail

Hidden Pond Trail

Tennessee Rock Trail

Nature Trail and Becky Branch Falls Trail

Wagon Train Trail

Sosebee Cove Trail

Gahuti Trail

Panther Creek Trail

Bradley Peak Trail

Blue Trail

West Palisades Trail

White Trail

Hall's Bridge Tract #1

River Bluff Trail

Ann Barber Wildflower Trail

Swamp Island Drive and Swamp Walk

Clam Creek Bicycle Path, Glory Path,
and St. Andrews Picnic Area

	MAR	APR	MAY	JUN	JUL	AUG	SEP	OCT

FLOWERING SEASON   PEAK FLOWERING

1
2
3
4
5
6
7
8
9
10
11
12
13
14
15
16
17
18
19
20

References

Brodo, I. M., S. D. Sharnoff, and S. Sharnoff. 2001. *Lichens of North America*. New Haven: Yale University Press.

Brown, C. L., and L. K. Kirkman. 1990. *Trees of Georgia and Surrounding States*. Portland, OR: Timber Press.

Brown, F., and N. Jones. 1996. *The Georgia Conservancy's Guide to the North Georgia Mountains*. 3rd ed. Atlanta: Longstreet Press.

Bruddell, G. F., III, and J. W. Thieret. 1985. Notes on *Erigenia bulbosa* (Apiaceae). *Bartonia*, no. 51:69–76.

Case, F. W., Jr., and R. B. Case. 1997. *Trilliums*. Portland, OR: Timber Press.

Coffey, T. 1993. *The History and Folklore of North American Wildflowers*. Boston, MA: Houghton Mifflin Company.

Costello, J. 2004. Personal communication.

Duncan, W., and M. B. Duncan. 1987. *The Smithsonian Guide to Seaside Plants of the Gulf and Atlantic Coasts*. Washington, DC: The Smithsonian Institution Press.

———. 1988. *Trees of the Southeastern United States*. Athens: University of Georgia Press.

———. 1999. *Wildflowers of the Eastern United States*. Athens: University of Georgia Press.

Duncan, W., and L. E. Foote. 1975. *Wildflowers of the Southeastern United States*. Athens: University of Georgia Press.

Edwards, L. 2004. *The Okefenokee Swamp*. http://www.gabotsoc.org; select Articles and then Places.

Emerson, V. 1986. Site-Seeing: Good Luck at Sosebee Cove. *Tipularia* 1(1):38.

Foote, L. E., and S. B. Jones, Jr. 1989. *Native Shrubs and Woody Vines of the Southeast*. Portland, OR: Timber Press.

Godfrey, R. K., and J. W. Wooten. 1979. *Aquatic and Wetland Plants of Southeastern United States, Monocotyledons*. Athens: University of Georgia Press.

———. 1981. *Aquatic and Wetland Plants of Southeastern United States, Dicotyledons*. Athens: University of Georgia Press.

Harper, F. 1998. *The Travels of William Bartram: Naturalist's Edition*. Athens: University of Georgia Press.

Harris, M. 2003. *Botanica North America*. New York: HarperResource.

Hicks, D. J., R. Wyatt, and T. R. Meagher. 1985. Reproductive Biology of Distylous Partridgeberry, *Mitchella Repens. Amer. J. Bot.* 72(10):1503–1514.

Homan, T. 1997. *The Hiking Trails of North Georgia*. 3rd ed. Atlanta: Peachtree.

Jones, S. B., Jr., and L. E. Foote. 1990. *Gardening with Native Wild Flowers*. Portland, OR: Timber Press.

Lampros, A., and D. Warner. *An Interpretive Guide to the Tennessee Rock Trail*. Mountain City, GA: Black Rock Mountain State Park.

Midgley, J. W. 1999. *Southeastern Wildflowers*. Birmingham, AL: Crane Hill Publishers.

Mitchell, S. 1999. Access Guide. The Natural Communities of Georgia. Longleaf Pine–Wiregrass Community. Joseph W. Jones Ecological Research Center, and Wildlife Resources Division of Georgia Department of Natural Resources.

Niering, W. A. 1979. *The Audubon Society Field Guide to North American Wildflowers*. Eastern Region. New York: Alfred A. Knopf.

Patrick, T. S., J. R. Allison, and G. A. Krakow. 1995. *Protected Plants of Georgia*. Social Circle, GA: Georgia Natural Heritage Program, Wildlife Resources Division, Georgia Department of Natural Resources.

Pfitzer, D. W. 1993. *The Hiker's Guide to Georgia*. Helena, MT: Falcon Press.

Porcher, R. D., and D. A. Rayner. 2001. *A Guide to the Wildflowers of South Carolina*. Columbia, SC: University of South Carolina Press.

Radford, A. E., H. E. Ahles, and C. R. Bell. 1968. *Manual of the Vascular Flora of the Carolinas*. Chapel Hill, NC: University of North Carolina Press.

Rickett, H. W. 1966. *Wild Flowers of the United States, The Southeastern States*. 2 vols. New York: McGraw-Hill.

Schoettle, T. 1996. *A Guide to a Georgia Barrier Island*. St. Simons Island, GA: Watermarks Publishing.

———. 2002. *A Naturalist's Guide to the Okefenokee Swamp*. Darien, GA: Darien Printing and Graphics.

Snyder, L. H., and J. G. Bruce. 1986. *Field Guide to the Ferns*. Athens: University of Georgia Press.

Van Horn, G. S. 1981. A Checklist of the Vascular Plants of Chickamauga and Chattanooga National Military Park. *Journal of the Tennessee Academy of Science* 56:92–99.

———. 1991. Cedar Glades of Northwest Georgia. *Tipularia* 5(1):22–27.

Weakley, A. S. 2005. *Flora of the Carolinas, Virginia, and Georgia.* Draft, Mar. 4, 2005. www.herbarium.unc.edu.

Wharton, C. H. 1978. The Natural Environments of Georgia. Bulletin 114. Atlanta: Geologic and Water Resources Division and Resource Planning Section, Office of Planning and Research, Georgia Department of Natural Resources.

Wyatt, R., and J. R. Allison. 2000. Flora and Vegetation of Granite Outcrops in the Southeastern United States. In *Inselbergs,* ed. S. Porembski and W. Barthlott. Vol. 146, Ecological Studies. Berlin: Springer-Verlag.

Index

Page numbers in **bold** type refer to a profile and photo.

buckeye (*Aesculus* sp.)
  Ohio (*A. glabra*), 5
  painted (*A. sylvatica*), 30, 119
  red (*A. pavia*), 27, 114
  yellow (*A. flava*), 2, 68
bugbane
  American (*Actaea podocarpa*), 46
  false (*Trautvetteria carolinensis*), 63, 67
bunchflower (*Veratrum latifolium*), 91
bur-marigold (*Bidens laevis*), 153
bush, strawberry (*Euonymus americanus*),
  22, 24, 31, 55, 90, 114, 123
buttercup (*Ranunculus* sp.), 29, 71, 134
  hooked (*R. recurvatus*), 55
butterwort, violet (*Pinguicula caerulea*), 152
button
  bachelor's (*Polygala nana*), 144
  bog (*Lachnocaulon anceps*), 143

Cacalia atriplicifolia. See *Arnoglossom
  atriplicifolium*
Cakile edentula (sea-rocket), **162**, 163
Calamintha sp. See *Clinopodium* sp.
Calopogon barbatus (grass-pink), 152
Calycanthus floridus (sweet-shrub), 17, 18,
  30, 31, 55, 76, 114
Camassia scilloides (wild hyacinth), 6, 7,
  34, 37
Campanula divaricata (southern harebell),
  24, 45, 59, 71, 82, 123
camphorweed (*Heterotheca subaxillaris*),
  163
campion, starry (*Silene stellata*), 123
Canada-mayflower (*Maianthemum
  canadense*), 63, **64**
candyweed (*Polygala lutea*), 144, 147, 152
cane (*Arundinaria gigantea*), 102
Cardamine
  concatenata (cutleaf toothwort), 4,
    133, **136**

diphylla (toothwort), 4, 17, 27, 63,
  71, 112
dissecta (dissected toothwort), 34
carphephorus (*Carphephorus* sp.), 147
Carphephorus sp. (carphephorus), 147
Carpinus caroliniana (American
  hornbeam), 2, 25, 133
Carya sp. (hickory), 17, 84
Castanea dentata (American chestnut), 45
Caulophyllum thalictroides (blue cohosh),
  5, 46, 71
Ceanothus americanus (New Jersey tea),
  24, 31, 56, 57
cedar, eastern red. *See* redcedar, eastern
celandine-poppy (*Stylophorum diphyllum*),
  4, **8**
Ceratiola ericoides (sandhill rosemary),
  127, **130**
Chamaecrista fasciculata (partridge-pea),
  122
Chamaelirium luteum (devil's-bit), **30**,
  31, 85
Chaptalia tomentosa (sunbonnets), 142
Chasmanthium sessiliflorum (woodoats),
  102
Cheilanthes lanosa (hairy lipfern), 106
Chelone glabra (turtlehead), **21**, 24, 38, 91
chestnut, American (*Castanea dentata*), 45
chickweed, giant (*Stellaria pubera*), 5, 17,
  18, 27, 54, 71, 78, **113**, 114, 119
Chimaphila maculata (pipsissewa), **22**, 23,
  46, 56, 81, 90, 114, 122
chokeberry, black (*Aronia melanocarpa*),
  66
Chrysogonum virginianum (green-and-
  gold), 85, **87**, 112, 117
Chrysoma pauciflosculosa (bush goldenrod),
  127, 130, **131**, 132
Chrysopsis mariana (golden-aster), 24, 33,
  115, 123
cicely, sweet (*Osmorhiza claytonii*), 71